Enterprise Technology
Complete Self-Assessment Guide

The guidance in this Self-Assessment is based on best practices and standards in business process and quality management. The guidance is also based on the professional judgment of the individual collaborators listed in the Acknowledgments.

Notice of rights

Copyright © by The Art of Service
http://theartofservice.com
service@theartofservice.com

Table of Contents

About The Art of Service

The Art of Service, Business Process Architects since 2000, is dedicated to helping stakeholders achieve excellence.

Defining, designing, creating, and implementing a process to solve a stakeholders challenge or meet an objective is the most valuable role... In EVERY group, company, organization and department.

Unless you're talking a one-time, single-use project, there should be a process. Whether that process is managed and implemented by humans, AI, or a combination of the two, it needs to be designed by someone with a complex enough perspective to ask the right questions.

Someone capable of asking the right questions and step back and say, 'What are we really trying to accomplish here? And is there a different way to look at it?'

With The Art of Service's Standard Requirements Self-Assessments, we empower people who can do just that — whether their title is marketer, entrepreneur, manager, salesperson, consultant, Business Process Manager, executive assistant, IT Manager, CIO etc... —they are the people who rule the future. They are people who watch the process as it happens, and ask the right questions to make the process work better.

Contact us when you need any support with this Self-Assessment and any help with templates, blue-prints and examples of standard documents you might need:

http://theartofservice.com
service@theartofservice.com

Acknowledgments

This checklist was developed under the auspices of The Art of Service, chaired by Gerardus Blokdyk.

Representatives from several client companies participated in the preparation of this Self-Assessment.

In addition, we are thankful for the design and printing services provided.

Included Resources - how to access

Included with your purchase of the book is the Enterprise Technology Self-Assessment Spreadsheet Dashboard which contains all questions and Self-Assessment areas and auto-generates insights, graphs, and project RACI planning - all with examples to get you started right away.

How? Simply send an email to
access@theartofservice.com
with this books' title in the subject to get the Enterprise Technology Self Assessment Tool right away.

You will receive the following contents with New and Updated specific criteria:

- The latest quick edition of the book in PDF

- The latest complete edition of the book in PDF, which criteria correspond to the criteria in...

- The Self-Assessment Excel Dashboard, and...

- Example pre-filled Self-Assessment Excel Dashboard to get familiar with results generation

- In-depth specific Checklists covering the topic

- Project management checklists and templates to assist with implementation

INCLUDES LIFETIME SELF ASSESSMENT UPDATES

Every self assessment comes with Lifetime Updates and Lifetime Free Updated Books. Lifetime Updates is an industry-first feature which allows you to receive verified self assessment updates, ensuring you always have the most accurate information at your fingertips.

Get it now- you will be glad you did - do it now, before you forget.

Send an email to **access@theartofservice.com** with this books' title in the subject to get the Enterprise Technology Self Assessment Tool right away.

Your feedback is invaluable to us

If you recently bought this book, we would love to hear from you! You can do this by writing a review on amazon (or the online store where you purchased this book) about your last purchase! As part of our continual service improvement process, we love to hear real client experiences and feedback.

How does it work?
To post a review on Amazon, just log in to your account and click on the Create Your Own Review button (under Customer Reviews) of the relevant product page. You can find examples of product reviews in Amazon. If you purchased from another online store, simply follow their procedures.

What happens when I submit my review?
Once you have submitted your review, send us an email at review@theartofservice.com with the link to your review so we can properly thank you for your feedback.

Purpose of this Self-Assessment

This Self-Assessment has been developed to improve understanding of the requirements and elements of Enterprise Technology, based on best practices and standards in business process architecture, design and quality management.

It is designed to allow for a rapid Self-Assessment to determine how closely existing management practices and procedures correspond to the elements of the Self-Assessment.

The criteria of requirements and elements of Enterprise Technology have been rephrased in the format of a Self-Assessment questionnaire, with a seven-criterion scoring system, as explained in this document.

In this format, even with limited background knowledge of

Enterprise Technology, a manager can quickly review existing operations to determine how they measure up to the standards. This in turn can serve as the starting point of a 'gap analysis' to identify management tools or system elements that might usefully be implemented in the organization to help improve overall performance.

How to use the Self-Assessment

On the following pages are a series of questions to identify to what extent your Enterprise Technology initiative is complete in comparison to the requirements set in standards.

To facilitate answering the questions, there is a space in front of each question to enter a score on a scale of '1' to '5'.

1 Strongly Disagree

2 Disagree

3 Neutral

4 Agree

5 Strongly Agree

Read the question and rate it with the following in front of mind:

'In my belief, the answer to this question is clearly defined'.

There are two ways in which you can choose to interpret this statement;
1. how aware are you that the answer to the question is clearly defined
2. for more in-depth analysis you can choose to gather

evidence and confirm the answer to the question. This obviously will take more time, most Self-Assessment users opt for the first way to interpret the question and dig deeper later on based on the outcome of the overall Self-Assessment.

A score of '1' would mean that the answer is not clear at all, where a '5' would mean the answer is crystal clear and defined. Leave emtpy when the question is not applicable or you don't want to answer it, you can skip it without affecting your score. Write your score in the space provided.

After you have responded to all the appropriate statements in each section, compute your average score for that section, using the formula provided, and round to the nearest tenth. Then transfer to the corresponding spoke in the Enterprise Technology Scorecard on the second next page of the Self-Assessment.

Your completed Enterprise Technology Scorecard will give you a clear presentation of which Enterprise Technology areas need attention.

Enterprise Technology Scorecard Example

Example of how the finalized Scorecard can look like:

Enterprise Technology Scorecard

Your Scores:

BEGINNING OF THE SELF-ASSESSMENT:

CRITERION #1: RECOGNIZE

INTENT: Be aware of the need for change. Recognize that there is an unfavorable variation, problem or symptom.

In my belief, the answer to this question is clearly defined:

5 Strongly Agree

4 Agree

3 Neutral

2 Disagree

1 Strongly Disagree

1. Are employees recognized for desired behaviors?
<--- Score

2. Do you need different information or graphics?
<--- Score

3. What are the Enterprise Technology resources needed?
<--- Score

4. Will it solve real problems?
<--- Score

5. How many trainings, in total, are needed?
<--- Score

6. What is the problem and/or vulnerability?
<--- Score

7. How are training requirements identified?
<--- Score

8. Does the problem have ethical dimensions?
<--- Score

9. What should be considered when identifying available resources, constraints, and deadlines?
<--- Score

10. What are the minority interests and what amount of minority interests can be recognized?
<--- Score

11. Is the quality assurance team identified?
<--- Score

12. How can auditing be a preventative security measure?
<--- Score

13. Would you recognize a threat from the inside?
<--- Score

14. Which issues are too important to ignore?
<--- Score

15. Are there regulatory / compliance issues?
<--- Score

16. Who needs to know?
<--- Score

17. Have you identified your Enterprise Technology key performance indicators?
<--- Score

18. What creative shifts do you need to take?
<--- Score

19. How does it fit into your organizational needs and tasks?
<--- Score

20. Are you dealing with any of the same issues today as yesterday? What can you do about this?
<--- Score

21. What is the smallest subset of the problem you can usefully solve?
<--- Score

22. Are there Enterprise Technology problems defined?
<--- Score

23. Who defines the rules in relation to any given issue?
<--- Score

24. Does Enterprise Technology create potential expectations in other areas that need to be

recognized and considered?
<--- Score

25. Is it clear when you think of the day ahead of you what activities and tasks you need to complete?
<--- Score

26. To what extent would your organization benefit from being recognized as a award recipient?
<--- Score

27. What Enterprise Technology coordination do you need?
<--- Score

28. Can management personnel recognize the monetary benefit of Enterprise Technology?
<--- Score

29. Do you know what you need to know about Enterprise Technology?
<--- Score

30. How are you going to measure success?
<--- Score

31. Do you need to avoid or amend any Enterprise Technology activities?
<--- Score

32. Will new equipment/products be required to facilitate Enterprise Technology delivery, for example is new software needed?
<--- Score

33. Are problem definition and motivation clearly

presented?
<--- Score

34. What prevents you from making the changes you know will make you a more effective Enterprise Technology leader?
<--- Score

35. What problems are you facing and how do you consider Enterprise Technology will circumvent those obstacles?
<--- Score

36. Which needs are not included or involved?
<--- Score

37. What do you need to start doing?
<--- Score

38. What resources or support might you need?
<--- Score

39. How do you identify the kinds of information that you will need?
<--- Score

40. Where do you need to exercise leadership?
<--- Score

41. Does your organization need more Enterprise Technology education?
<--- Score

42. Did you miss any major Enterprise Technology issues?
<--- Score

43. Are controls defined to recognize and contain problems?
<--- Score

44. What is the problem or issue?
<--- Score

45. How do you recognize an Enterprise Technology objection?
<--- Score

46. What does Enterprise Technology success mean to the stakeholders?
<--- Score

47. How do you assess your Enterprise Technology workforce capability and capacity needs, including skills, competencies, and staffing levels?
<--- Score

48. What Enterprise Technology capabilities do you need?
<--- Score

49. Who needs what information?
<--- Score

50. Do you recognize Enterprise Technology achievements?
<--- Score

51. What situation(s) led to this Enterprise Technology Self Assessment?
<--- Score

52. What needs to be done?
<--- Score

53. Do you have/need 24-hour access to key personnel?
<--- Score

54. What do employees need in the short term?
<--- Score

55. What are the clients issues and concerns?
<--- Score

56. Whom do you really need or want to serve?
<--- Score

57. Are your goals realistic? Do you need to redefine your problem? Perhaps the problem has changed or maybe you have reached your goal and need to set a new one?
<--- Score

58. Looking at each person individually – does every one have the qualities which are needed to work in this group?
<--- Score

59. What else needs to be measured?
<--- Score

60. Are there any revenue recognition issues?
<--- Score

61. What is the Enterprise Technology problem definition? What do you need to resolve?
<--- Score

62. Is it needed?
<--- Score

63. What Enterprise Technology problem should be solved?
<--- Score

64. Where is training needed?
<--- Score

65. Who else hopes to benefit from it?
<--- Score

66. How are the Enterprise Technology's objectives aligned to the group's overall stakeholder strategy?
<--- Score

67. What are the expected benefits of Enterprise Technology to the stakeholder?
<--- Score

68. What activities does the governance board need to consider?
<--- Score

69. Are there any specific expectations or concerns about the Enterprise Technology team, Enterprise Technology itself?
<--- Score

70. As a sponsor, customer or management, how important is it to meet goals, objectives?
<--- Score

71. How do you recognize an objection?

<--- Score

72. Think about the people you identified for your Enterprise Technology project and the project responsibilities you would assign to them, what kind of training do you think they would need to perform these responsibilities effectively?
<--- Score

73. Are there recognized Enterprise Technology problems?
<--- Score

74. Will a response program recognize when a crisis occurs and provide some level of response?
<--- Score

75. What are your needs in relation to Enterprise Technology skills, labor, equipment, and markets?
<--- Score

76. To what extent does each concerned units management team recognize Enterprise Technology as an effective investment?
<--- Score

77. What would happen if Enterprise Technology weren't done?
<--- Score

78. What needs to stay?
<--- Score

79. What are the timeframes required to resolve each of the issues/problems?
<--- Score

80. What Enterprise Technology events should you attend?
<--- Score

81. Which information does the Enterprise Technology business case need to include?
<--- Score

82. For your Enterprise Technology project, identify and describe the business environment, is there more than one layer to the business environment?
<--- Score

83. How much are sponsors, customers, partners, stakeholders involved in Enterprise Technology? In other words, what are the risks, if Enterprise Technology does not deliver successfully?
<--- Score

84. Who needs budgets?
<--- Score

85. Is the need for organizational change recognized?
<--- Score

86. What training and capacity building actions are needed to implement proposed reforms?
<--- Score

87. What information do users need?
<--- Score

88. Will Enterprise Technology deliverables need to be tested and, if so, by whom?
<--- Score

89. What tools and technologies are needed for a custom Enterprise Technology project?
<--- Score

90. Are employees recognized or rewarded for performance that demonstrates the highest levels of integrity?
<--- Score

91. Who are your key stakeholders who need to sign off?
<--- Score

92. Who needs to know about Enterprise Technology?
<--- Score

93. How do you identify subcontractor relationships?
<--- Score

94. What vendors make products that address the Enterprise Technology needs?
<--- Score

95. Who should resolve the Enterprise Technology issues?
<--- Score

96. What are the stakeholder objectives to be achieved with Enterprise Technology?
<--- Score

97. Why the need?
<--- Score

Add up total points for this section:

_____ = Total points for this section

Divided by: _____ (number of
statements answered) = _____
Average score for this section

Transfer your score to the Enterprise
Technology Index at the beginning of
the Self-Assessment.

CRITERION #2: DEFINE:

1. Are team charters developed?
<--- Score

2. How do you manage scope?
<--- Score

3. Is there a clear Enterprise Technology case definition?
<--- Score

4. Where can you gather more information?
<--- Score

5. Have the customer needs been translated into specific, measurable requirements? How?
<--- Score

6. Have all of the relationships been defined properly?
<--- Score

7. When are meeting minutes sent out? Who is on the distribution list?
<--- Score

8. How do you gather Enterprise Technology requirements?
<--- Score

9. Has/have the customer(s) been identified?
<--- Score

10. What are the compelling stakeholder reasons for embarking on Enterprise Technology?
<--- Score

11. Has anyone else (internal or external to the group) attempted to solve this problem or a similar one before? If so, what knowledge can be leveraged from these previous efforts?
<--- Score

12. Are all requirements met?
<--- Score

13. How does the Enterprise Technology manager

ensure against scope creep?
<--- Score

14. Is full participation by members in regularly held team meetings guaranteed?
<--- Score

15. Is the scope of Enterprise Technology defined?
<--- Score

16. How do you manage unclear Enterprise Technology requirements?
<--- Score

17. Are improvement team members fully trained on Enterprise Technology?
<--- Score

18. What is the scope of Enterprise Technology?
<--- Score

19. What are the tasks and definitions?
<--- Score

20. Is there a Enterprise Technology management charter, including stakeholder case, problem and goal statements, scope, milestones, roles and responsibilities, communication plan?
<--- Score

21. Are roles and responsibilities formally defined?
<--- Score

22. Are there different segments of customers?
<--- Score

23. What Enterprise Technology requirements should be gathered?
<--- Score

24. Is the team equipped with available and reliable resources?
<--- Score

25. What Enterprise Technology services do you require?
<--- Score

26. Is Enterprise Technology currently on schedule according to the plan?
<--- Score

27. Has a team charter been developed and communicated?
<--- Score

28. What would be the goal or target for a Enterprise Technology's improvement team?
<--- Score

29. Do you have organizational privacy requirements?
<--- Score

30. Are customers identified and high impact areas defined?
<--- Score

31. Will a Enterprise Technology production readiness review be required?
<--- Score

32. What is the worst case scenario?

<--- Score

33. Who are the Enterprise Technology improvement
team members, including Management Leads and
Coaches?
<--- Score

34. Why are you doing Enterprise Technology and
what is the scope?
<--- Score

35. What is out-of-scope initially?
<--- Score

36. Has a Enterprise Technology requirement not been
met?
<--- Score

37. How will variation in the actual durations of each
activity be dealt with to ensure that the expected
Enterprise Technology results are met?
<--- Score

38. What are the boundaries of the scope? What is in
bounds and what is not? What is the start point? What
is the stop point?
<--- Score

39. Are the Enterprise Technology requirements
complete?
<--- Score

40. If substitutes have been appointed, have they
been briefed on the Enterprise Technology goals and
received regular communications as to the progress
to date?

<--- Score

41. Who is gathering Enterprise Technology information?
<--- Score

42. In what way can you redefine the criteria of choice clients have in your category in your favor?
<--- Score

43. What are the Enterprise Technology use cases?
<--- Score

44. What is the scope of the Enterprise Technology work?
<--- Score

45. Is the improvement team aware of the different versions of a process: what they think it is vs. what it actually is vs. what it should be vs. what it could be?
<--- Score

46. Do you have a Enterprise Technology success story or case study ready to tell and share?
<--- Score

47. What are the core elements of the Enterprise Technology business case?
<--- Score

48. Is the Enterprise Technology scope complete and appropriately sized?
<--- Score

49. What is in the scope and what is not in scope?
<--- Score

50. What is out of scope?
<--- Score

51. How do you catch Enterprise Technology definition inconsistencies?
<--- Score

52. The political context: who holds power?
<--- Score

53. Is Enterprise Technology linked to key stakeholder goals and objectives?
<--- Score

54. What customer feedback methods were used to solicit their input?
<--- Score

55. How would you define Enterprise Technology leadership?
<--- Score

56. What is a worst-case scenario for losses?
<--- Score

57. Is the team adequately staffed with the desired cross-functionality? If not, what additional resources are available to the team?
<--- Score

58. Are stakeholder processes mapped?
<--- Score

59. What is the context?
<--- Score

60. Is the Enterprise Technology scope manageable?
<--- Score

61. What specifically is the problem? Where does it occur? When does it occur? What is its extent?
<--- Score

62. What critical content must be communicated – who, what, when, where, and how?
<--- Score

63. Has a high-level 'as is' process map been completed, verified and validated?
<--- Score

64. Are required metrics defined, what are they?
<--- Score

65. What are (control) requirements for Enterprise Technology Information?
<--- Score

66. What information do you gather?
<--- Score

67. Is scope creep really all bad news?
<--- Score

68. Have specific policy objectives been defined?
<--- Score

69. Are resources adequate for the scope?
<--- Score

70. When is the estimated completion date?

<--- Score

71. Will team members perform Enterprise Technology work when assigned and in a timely fashion?
<--- Score

72. Is there a critical path to deliver Enterprise Technology results?
<--- Score

73. What is the definition of Enterprise Technology excellence?
<--- Score

74. Does the team have regular meetings?
<--- Score

75. Is there any additional Enterprise Technology definition of success?
<--- Score

76. What is the scope of the Enterprise Technology effort?
<--- Score

77. How do you hand over Enterprise Technology context?
<--- Score

78. Are approval levels defined for contracts and supplements to contracts?
<--- Score

79. What are the dynamics of the communication plan?
<--- Score

80. How will the Enterprise Technology team and the group measure complete success of Enterprise Technology?
<--- Score

81. Does the scope remain the same?
<--- Score

82. How are consistent Enterprise Technology definitions important?
<--- Score

83. What key stakeholder process output measure(s) does Enterprise Technology leverage and how?
<--- Score

84. Do you all define Enterprise Technology in the same way?
<--- Score

85. Is the team sponsored by a champion or stakeholder leader?
<--- Score

86. What are the Roles and Responsibilities for each team member and its leadership? Where is this documented?
<--- Score

87. Has a project plan, Gantt chart, or similar been developed/completed?
<--- Score

88. How do you build the right business case?
<--- Score

89. Is the current 'as is' process being followed? If not, what are the discrepancies?
<--- Score

90. Are accountability and ownership for Enterprise Technology clearly defined?
<--- Score

91. Who approved the Enterprise Technology scope?
<--- Score

92. What was the context?
<--- Score

93. What happens if Enterprise Technology's scope changes?
<--- Score

94. What information should you gather?
<--- Score

95. What are the rough order estimates on cost savings/opportunities that Enterprise Technology brings?
<--- Score

96. How do you manage changes in Enterprise Technology requirements?
<--- Score

97. What is in scope?
<--- Score

98. Has the Enterprise Technology work been fairly and/or equitably divided and delegated among team

members who are qualified and capable to perform the work? Has everyone contributed?
<--- Score

99. Will team members regularly document their Enterprise Technology work?
<--- Score

100. Has the improvement team collected the 'voice of the customer' (obtained feedback – qualitative and quantitative)?
<--- Score

101. Has everyone on the team, including the team leaders, been properly trained?
<--- Score

102. How do you keep key subject matter experts in the loop?
<--- Score

103. Is it clearly defined in and to your organization what you do?
<--- Score

104. What defines best in class?
<--- Score

105. How do you think the partners involved in Enterprise Technology would have defined success?
<--- Score

106. Who is gathering information?
<--- Score

107. How and when will the baselines be defined?

<--- Score

108. Has the direction changed at all during the course of Enterprise Technology? If so, when did it change and why?
<--- Score

109. What intelligence can you gather?
<--- Score

110. How often are the team meetings?
<--- Score

111. How would you define the culture at your organization, how susceptible is it to Enterprise Technology changes?
<--- Score

112. Are audit criteria, scope, frequency and methods defined?
<--- Score

113. What baselines are required to be defined and managed?
<--- Score

114. Are there any constraints known that bear on the ability to perform Enterprise Technology work? How is the team addressing them?
<--- Score

115. How was the 'as is' process map developed, reviewed, verified and validated?
<--- Score

116. What are the requirements for audit information?

<--- Score

117. What scope do you want your strategy to cover?
<--- Score

118. How did the Enterprise Technology manager receive input to the development of a Enterprise Technology improvement plan and the estimated completion dates/times of each activity?
<--- Score

119. How is the team tracking and documenting its work?
<--- Score

120. What system do you use for gathering Enterprise Technology information?
<--- Score

121. Who defines (or who defined) the rules and roles?
<--- Score

122. What are the Enterprise Technology tasks and definitions?
<--- Score

123. How have you defined all Enterprise Technology requirements first?
<--- Score

124. When is/was the Enterprise Technology start date?
<--- Score

125. Is there regularly 100% attendance at the team meetings? If not, have appointed substitutes

attended to preserve cross-functionality and full representation?

<--- Score

126. What sources do you use to gather information for a Enterprise Technology study?

<--- Score

127. Are the Enterprise Technology requirements testable?

<--- Score

128. Are task requirements clearly defined?

<--- Score

129. Is Enterprise Technology required?

<--- Score

130. What scope to assess?

<--- Score

131. Is there a completed SIPOC representation, describing the Suppliers, Inputs, Process, Outputs, and Customers?

<--- Score

132. Scope of sensitive information?

<--- Score

133. How do you gather requirements?

<--- Score

134. Are customer(s) identified and segmented according to their different needs and requirements?

<--- Score

135. Is the team formed and are team leaders (Coaches and Management Leads) assigned?
<--- Score

136. Is a fully trained team formed, supported, and committed to work on the Enterprise Technology improvements?
<--- Score

137. What sort of initial information to gather?
<--- Score

138. How can the value of Enterprise Technology be defined?
<--- Score

139. Is data collected and displayed to better understand customer(s) critical needs and requirements.
<--- Score

140. Do the problem and goal statements meet the SMART criteria (specific, measurable, attainable, relevant, and time-bound)?
<--- Score

141. Are different versions of process maps needed to account for the different types of inputs?
<--- Score

142. What constraints exist that might impact the team?
<--- Score

143. What gets examined?
<--- Score

144. Is there a completed, verified, and validated high-level 'as is' (not 'should be' or 'could be') stakeholder process map?
<--- Score

Add up total points for this section:
_____ = Total points for this section

Divided by: _____ (number of statements answered) = _____
Average score for this section

Transfer your score to the Enterprise Technology Index at the beginning of the Self-Assessment.

CRITERION #3: MEASURE:

INTENT: Gather the correct data.
Measure the current performance and
evolution of the situation.

In my belief, the answer to this
question is clearly defined:

5 Strongly Agree

4 Agree

3 Neutral

2 Disagree

1 Strongly Disagree

1. How do you identify and analyze stakeholders and their interests?
<--- Score

2. How do you verify if Enterprise Technology is built right?
<--- Score

3. Have design-to-cost goals been established?

<--- Score

4. What key measures identified indicate the performance of the stakeholder process?
<--- Score

5. What are your key Enterprise Technology organizational performance measures, including key short and longer-term financial measures?
<--- Score

6. Is there an opportunity to verify requirements?
<--- Score

7. Which Enterprise Technology impacts are significant?
<--- Score

8. How do you measure lifecycle phases?
<--- Score

9. Do you have any cost Enterprise Technology limitation requirements?
<--- Score

10. How much does it cost?
<--- Score

11. What are your key Enterprise Technology indicators that you will measure, analyze and track?
<--- Score

12. How do you verify your resources?
<--- Score

13. What methods are feasible and acceptable to

estimate the impact of reforms?
<--- Score

14. How can you reduce costs?
<--- Score

15. Are high impact defects defined and identified in the stakeholder process?
<--- Score

16. Do staff have the necessary skills to collect, analyze, and report data?
<--- Score

17. What charts has the team used to display the components of variation in the process?
<--- Score

18. Where can you go to verify the info?
<--- Score

19. How is progress measured?
<--- Score

20. Do you have an issue in getting priority?
<--- Score

21. How do you stay flexible and focused to recognize larger Enterprise Technology results?
<--- Score

22. What can be used to verify compliance?
<--- Score

23. When is Root Cause Analysis Required?
<--- Score

24. Is a solid data collection plan established that includes measurement systems analysis?
<--- Score

25. What are the estimated costs of proposed changes?
<--- Score

26. What are the Enterprise Technology key cost drivers?
<--- Score

27. Do the benefits outweigh the costs?
<--- Score

28. What is an unallowable cost?
<--- Score

29. How is performance measured?
<--- Score

30. Was a life-cycle cost analysis performed?
<--- Score

31. Are you aware of what could cause a problem?
<--- Score

32. Is data collection planned and executed?
<--- Score

33. Are key measures identified and agreed upon?
<--- Score

34. What drives O&M cost?
<--- Score

35. What evidence is there and what is measured?
<--- Score

36. How do you quantify and qualify impacts?
<--- Score

37. What causes innovation to fail or succeed in your organization?
<--- Score

38. Do you verify that corrective actions were taken?
<--- Score

39. What are your primary costs, revenues, assets?
<--- Score

40. Who pays the cost?
<--- Score

41. How do you verify the Enterprise Technology requirements quality?
<--- Score

42. Does the Enterprise Technology task fit the client's priorities?
<--- Score

43. Does your organization systematically track and analyze outcomes related for accountability and quality improvement?
<--- Score

44. Are missed Enterprise Technology opportunities costing your organization money?
<--- Score

45. Is long term and short term variability accounted for?

<--- Score

46. Are there competing Enterprise Technology priorities?

<--- Score

47. What is measured? Why?

<--- Score

48. How large is the gap between current performance and the customer-specified (goal) performance?

<--- Score

49. Have you found any 'ground fruit' or 'low-hanging fruit' for immediate remedies to the gap in performance?

<--- Score

50. How do you control the overall costs of your work processes?

<--- Score

51. Why a Enterprise Technology focus?

<--- Score

52. Who should receive measurement reports?

<--- Score

53. How do you focus on what is right -not who is right?

<--- Score

54. What do you measure and why?
<--- Score

55. What causes investor action?
<--- Score

56. How does cost-to-serve analysis help?
<--- Score

57. How sensitive must the Enterprise Technology strategy be to cost?
<--- Score

58. Are you taking your company in the direction of better and revenue or cheaper and cost?
<--- Score

59. What tests verify requirements?
<--- Score

60. How frequently do you track Enterprise Technology measures?
<--- Score

61. Are there any easy-to-implement alternatives to Enterprise Technology? Sometimes other solutions are available that do not require the cost implications of a full-blown project?
<--- Score

62. How are costs allocated?
<--- Score

63. How will the Enterprise Technology data be analyzed?
<--- Score

64. How do you measure success?
<--- Score

65. Is it possible to estimate the impact of unanticipated complexity such as wrong or failed assumptions, feedback, etcetera on proposed reforms?
<--- Score

66. When a disaster occurs, who gets priority?
<--- Score

67. How are measurements made?
<--- Score

68. Are process variation components displayed/ communicated using suitable charts, graphs, plots?
<--- Score

69. Are the measurements objective?
<--- Score

70. Does a Enterprise Technology quantification method exist?
<--- Score

71. Are there measurements based on task performance?
<--- Score

72. Why do you expend time and effort to implement measurement, for whom?
<--- Score

73. What is the total fixed cost?

<--- Score

74. What details are required of the Enterprise Technology cost structure?
<--- Score

75. When should you bother with diagrams?
<--- Score

76. How do you know that any Enterprise Technology analysis is complete and comprehensive?
<--- Score

77. Is the scope of Enterprise Technology cost analysis cost-effective?
<--- Score

78. Does Enterprise Technology analysis isolate the fundamental causes of problems?
<--- Score

79. Is Process Variation Displayed/Communicated?
<--- Score

80. How do you measure efficient delivery of Enterprise Technology services?
<--- Score

81. How do your measurements capture actionable Enterprise Technology information for use in exceeding your customers expectations and securing your customers engagement?
<--- Score

82. What do people want to verify?
<--- Score

83. Are indirect costs charged to the Enterprise Technology program?
<--- Score

84. Was a data collection plan established?
<--- Score

85. What are the agreed upon definitions of the high impact areas, defect(s), unit(s), and opportunities that will figure into the process capability metrics?
<--- Score

86. Are actual costs in line with budgeted costs?
<--- Score

87. Why do the measurements/indicators matter?
<--- Score

88. Have the types of risks that may impact Enterprise Technology been identified and analyzed?
<--- Score

89. Is the solution cost-effective?
<--- Score

90. How frequently do you verify your Enterprise Technology strategy?
<--- Score

91. What are allowable costs?
<--- Score

92. What could cause you to change course?
<--- Score

93. How can you manage cost down?
<--- Score

94. How do you verify performance?
<--- Score

95. What disadvantage does this cause for the user?
<--- Score

96. Where is the cost?
<--- Score

97. What causes extra work or rework?
<--- Score

98. What are the key input variables? What are the key process variables? What are the key output variables?
<--- Score

99. What is your decision requirements diagram?
<--- Score

100. What are the costs of delaying Enterprise Technology action?
<--- Score

101. Are the Enterprise Technology benefits worth its costs?
<--- Score

102. What causes mismanagement?
<--- Score

103. Have all non-recommended alternatives been analyzed in sufficient detail?
<--- Score

104. Was a business case (cost/benefit) developed?
<--- Score

105. What are your customers expectations and measures?
<--- Score

106. At what cost?
<--- Score

107. What is the right balance of time and resources between investigation, analysis, and discussion and dissemination?
<--- Score

108. What relevant entities could be measured?
<--- Score

109. Do you aggressively reward and promote the people who have the biggest impact on creating excellent Enterprise Technology services/products?
<--- Score

110. Is there a Performance Baseline?
<--- Score

111. How can you reduce the costs of obtaining inputs?
<--- Score

112. What are hidden Enterprise Technology quality costs?
<--- Score

113. What is the total cost related to deploying

Enterprise Technology, including any consulting or professional services?
<--- Score

114. How can a Enterprise Technology test verify your ideas or assumptions?
<--- Score

115. How do you prevent mis-estimating cost?
<--- Score

116. Is a follow-up focused external Enterprise Technology review required?
<--- Score

117. How do you verify the authenticity of the data and information used?
<--- Score

118. Which measures and indicators matter?
<--- Score

119. How will measures be used to manage and adapt?
<--- Score

120. Can you measure the return on analysis?
<--- Score

121. Have you made assumptions about the shape of the future, particularly its impact on your customers and competitors?
<--- Score

122. How can you measure Enterprise Technology in a systematic way?

<--- Score

123. Has a cost center been established?
<--- Score

124. How do you verify and develop ideas and innovations?
<--- Score

125. What would be a real cause for concern?
<--- Score

126. Do you effectively measure and reward individual and team performance?
<--- Score

127. What are the current costs of the Enterprise Technology process?
<--- Score

128. How can you measure the performance?
<--- Score

129. The approach of traditional Enterprise Technology works for detail complexity but is focused on a systematic approach rather than an understanding of the nature of systems themselves, what approach will permit your organization to deal with the kind of unpredictable emergent behaviors that dynamic complexity can introduce?
<--- Score

130. How will success or failure be measured?
<--- Score

131. How do you verify Enterprise Technology

completeness and accuracy?
<--- Score

132. What are your operating costs?
<--- Score

133. How do you do risk analysis of rare, cascading, catastrophic events?
<--- Score

134. Are you able to realize any cost savings?
<--- Score

135. How are you verifying it?
<--- Score

136. Among the Enterprise Technology product and service cost to be estimated, which is considered hardest to estimate?
<--- Score

137. What kind of analytics data will be gathered?
<--- Score

138. What measurements are being captured?
<--- Score

139. Are losses documented, analyzed, and remedial processes developed to prevent future losses?
<--- Score

140. Which stakeholder characteristics are analyzed?
<--- Score

141. Did you tackle the cause or the symptom?
<--- Score

142. What does a Test Case verify?
<--- Score

143. How do you measure variability?
<--- Score

144. Who is involved in verifying compliance?
<--- Score

145. What are the uncertainties surrounding estimates of impact?
<--- Score

146. Are supply costs steady or fluctuating?
<--- Score

147. How do you verify and validate the Enterprise Technology data?
<--- Score

148. How will effects be measured?
<--- Score

149. What harm might be caused?
<--- Score

150. What is the cause of any Enterprise Technology gaps?
<--- Score

151. Is data collected on key measures that were identified?
<--- Score

152. Do you have a flow diagram of what happens?

<--- Score

153. What measurements are possible, practicable and meaningful?
<--- Score

154. How will your organization measure success?
<--- Score

155. What could cause delays in the schedule?
<--- Score

156. What does losing customers cost your organization?
<--- Score

157. What are the costs?
<--- Score

158. How do you aggregate measures across priorities?
<--- Score

159. Have changes been properly/adequately analyzed for effect?
<--- Score

160. Have the concerns of stakeholders to help identify and define potential barriers been obtained and analyzed?
<--- Score

161. How will you measure your Enterprise Technology effectiveness?
<--- Score

162. Have you included everything in your Enterprise Technology cost models?
<--- Score

163. What potential environmental factors impact the Enterprise Technology effort?
<--- Score

164. Who participated in the data collection for measurements?
<--- Score

165. What are you verifying?
<--- Score

166. What are predictive Enterprise Technology analytics?
<--- Score

167. Does Enterprise Technology systematically track and analyze outcomes for accountability and quality improvement?
<--- Score

168. When are costs are incurred?
<--- Score

169. Where is it measured?
<--- Score

170. How to cause the change?
<--- Score

171. What happens if cost savings do not materialize?
<--- Score

172. Can you do Enterprise Technology without complex (expensive) analysis?
<--- Score

173. What does verifying compliance entail?
<--- Score

174. Is key measure data collection planned and executed, process variation displayed and communicated and performance baselined?
<--- Score

175. Has a cost benefit analysis been performed?
<--- Score

176. How will you measure success?
<--- Score

177. What data was collected (past, present, future/ongoing)?
<--- Score

178. What are the strategic priorities for this year?
<--- Score

179. What has the team done to assure the stability and accuracy of the measurement process?
<--- Score

180. What is your cost benefit analysis?
<--- Score

181. What particular quality tools did the team find helpful in establishing measurements?
<--- Score

182. Is the cost worth the Enterprise Technology effort
?
<--- Score

183. Are Enterprise Technology vulnerabilities
categorized and prioritized?
<--- Score

184. What is the cost of rework?
<--- Score

185. What is the root cause(s) of the problem?
<--- Score

186. How is the value delivered by Enterprise
Technology being measured?
<--- Score

187. What are the costs and benefits?
<--- Score

Add up total points for this section:
_ _ _ _ _   = Total points for this section

Divided by: _ _ _ _ _ _ (number of
statements answered) = _ _ _ _ _ _
Average score for this section

Transfer your score to the Enterprise
Technology Index at the beginning of
the Self-Assessment.

CRITERION #4: ANALYZE:

INTENT: Analyze causes, assumptions and hypotheses.

In my belief, the answer to this question is clearly defined:

5 Strongly Agree

4 Agree

3 Neutral

2 Disagree

1 Strongly Disagree

1. Do you understand your management processes today?
<--- Score

2. Is data and process analysis, root cause analysis and quantifying the gap/opportunity in place?
<--- Score

3. Think about the functions involved in your Enterprise Technology project, what processes flow

from these functions?
<--- Score

4. Record-keeping requirements flow from the records needed as inputs, outputs, controls and for transformation of a Enterprise Technology process, are the records needed as inputs to the Enterprise Technology process available?
<--- Score

5. Did any additional data need to be collected?
<--- Score

6. What are your current levels and trends in key Enterprise Technology measures or indicators of product and process performance that are important to and directly serve your customers?
<--- Score

7. Who will gather what data?
<--- Score

8. Are gaps between current performance and the goal performance identified?
<--- Score

9. What tools were used to narrow the list of possible causes?
<--- Score

10. Is the required Enterprise Technology data gathered?
<--- Score

11. What are your key performance measures or indicators and in-process measures for the control

and improvement of your Enterprise Technology processes?
<--- Score

12. What other organizational variables, such as reward systems or communication systems, affect the performance of this Enterprise Technology process?
<--- Score

13. Where is Enterprise Technology data gathered?
<--- Score

14. How can risk management be tied procedurally to process elements?
<--- Score

15. Did any value-added analysis or 'lean thinking' take place to identify some of the gaps shown on the 'as is' process map?
<--- Score

16. What are evaluation criteria for the output?
<--- Score

17. Which Enterprise Technology data should be retained?
<--- Score

18. What successful thing are you doing today that may be blinding you to new growth opportunities?
<--- Score

19. Do your leaders quickly bounce back from setbacks?
<--- Score

20. Do staff qualifications match your project?
<--- Score

21. What is your organizations process which leads to recognition of value generation?
<--- Score

22. What is the Enterprise Technology Driver?
<--- Score

23. What is your organizations system for selecting qualified vendors?
<--- Score

24. How are outputs preserved and protected?
<--- Score

25. What does the data say about the performance of the stakeholder process?
<--- Score

26. Is the Enterprise Technology process severely broken such that a re-design is necessary?
<--- Score

27. What process should you select for improvement?
<--- Score

28. How was the detailed process map generated, verified, and validated?
<--- Score

29. How many input/output points does it require?
<--- Score

30. Are Enterprise Technology changes recognized

early enough to be approved through the regular process?
<--- Score

31. How is the data gathered?
<--- Score

32. What is the complexity of the output produced?
<--- Score

33. Does the enterprise technology, processes and projects set direction for future growth?
<--- Score

34. What Enterprise Technology data do you gather or use now?
<--- Score

35. What did the team gain from developing a sub-process map?
<--- Score

36. Are your outputs consistent?
<--- Score

37. What is the Value Stream Mapping?
<--- Score

38. Who is involved with workflow mapping?
<--- Score

39. What are the necessary qualifications?
<--- Score

40. Identify an operational issue in your organization, for example, could a particular task be done more

quickly or more efficiently by Enterprise Technology?
<--- Score

41. Can you add value to the current Enterprise
Technology decision-making process (largely
qualitative) by incorporating uncertainty modeling
(more quantitative)?
<--- Score

**42. How will the enterprise technology
infrastructure support massive amounts of new
data gathered from RFID scans and route it to the
correct applications and business processes?**
<--- Score

43. How do you identify specific Enterprise
Technology investment opportunities and emerging
trends?
<--- Score

44. How is Enterprise Technology data gathered?
<--- Score

45. Are all staff in core Enterprise Technology subjects
Highly Qualified?
<--- Score

46. What qualifications are necessary?
<--- Score

47. What Enterprise Technology data should be
collected?
<--- Score

48. Is the suppliers process defined and controlled?
<--- Score

49. How will the Enterprise Technology data be captured?
<--- Score

50. Were Pareto charts (or similar) used to portray the 'heavy hitters' (or key sources of variation)?
<--- Score

51. Who gets your output?
<--- Score

52. How do you measure the operational performance of your key work systems and processes, including productivity, cycle time, and other appropriate measures of process effectiveness, efficiency, and innovation?
<--- Score

53. What are the Enterprise Technology business drivers?
<--- Score

54. Are you missing Enterprise Technology opportunities?
<--- Score

55. Do several people in different organizational units assist with the Enterprise Technology process?
<--- Score

56. Do you have the authority to produce the output?
<--- Score

57. What types of data do your Enterprise Technology indicators require?

<--- Score

58. What controls do you have in place to protect data?
<--- Score

59. Have the problem and goal statements been updated to reflect the additional knowledge gained from the analyze phase?
<--- Score

60. How is the way you as the leader think and process information affecting your organizational culture?
<--- Score

61. How do you use Enterprise Technology data and information to support organizational decision making and innovation?
<--- Score

62. Should you invest in industry-recognized qualifications?
<--- Score

63. How difficult is it to qualify what Enterprise Technology ROI is?
<--- Score

64. How do you define collaboration and team output?
<--- Score

65. What resources go in to get the desired output?
<--- Score

66. Has an output goal been set?

<--- Score

67. Are all team members qualified for all tasks?
<--- Score

68. What are the best opportunities for value improvement?
<--- Score

69. Was a detailed process map created to amplify critical steps of the 'as is' stakeholder process?
<--- Score

70. How do you implement and manage your work processes to ensure that they meet design requirements?
<--- Score

71. Is the final output clearly identified?
<--- Score

72. What methods do you use to gather Enterprise Technology data?
<--- Score

73. Were there any improvement opportunities identified from the process analysis?
<--- Score

74. Is the performance gap determined?
<--- Score

75. How will the change process be managed?
<--- Score

76. What are the disruptive Enterprise Technology

technologies that enable your organization to radically change your business processes?
<--- Score

77. What are your current levels and trends in key measures or indicators of Enterprise Technology product and process performance that are important to and directly serve your customers? How do these results compare with the performance of your competitors and other organizations with similar offerings?
<--- Score

78. What were the financial benefits resulting from any 'ground fruit or low-hanging fruit' (quick fixes)?
<--- Score

79. What is the cost of poor quality as supported by the team's analysis?
<--- Score

80. What is the output?
<--- Score

81. What other jobs or tasks affect the performance of the steps in the Enterprise Technology process?
<--- Score

82. Is the gap/opportunity displayed and communicated in financial terms?
<--- Score

83. What quality tools were used to get through the analyze phase?
<--- Score

84. What were the crucial 'moments of truth' on the process map?
<--- Score

85. Do your employees have the opportunity to do what they do best everyday?
<--- Score

86. What Enterprise Technology metrics are outputs of the process?
<--- Score

87. Has data output been validated?
<--- Score

88. How often will data be collected for measures?
<--- Score

89. What qualifications are needed?
<--- Score

90. How much data can be collected in the given timeframe?
<--- Score

91. Think about some of the processes you undertake within your organization, which do you own?
<--- Score

92. Who is involved in the management review process?
<--- Score

93. What are your outputs?
<--- Score

94. What tools were used to generate the list of possible causes?
<--- Score

95. Where is the data coming from to measure compliance?
<--- Score

96. What qualifies as competition?
<--- Score

97. Who owns what data?
<--- Score

98. Have any additional benefits been identified that will result from closing all or most of the gaps?
<--- Score

99. A compounding model resolution with available relevant data can often provide insight towards a solution methodology; which Enterprise Technology models, tools and techniques are necessary?
<--- Score

100. What output to create?
<--- Score

101. What kind of crime could a potential new hire have committed that would not only not disqualify him/her from being hired by your organization, but would actually indicate that he/she might be a particularly good fit?
<--- Score

102. Do your contracts/agreements contain data security obligations?

<--- Score

103. What training and qualifications will you need?
<--- Score

104. Who qualifies to gain access to data?
<--- Score

105. How is the Enterprise Technology Value Stream Mapping managed?
<--- Score

106. Do quality systems drive continuous improvement?
<--- Score

107. Was a cause-and-effect diagram used to explore the different types of causes (or sources of variation)?
<--- Score

108. What internal processes need improvement?
<--- Score

109. What conclusions were drawn from the team's data collection and analysis? How did the team reach these conclusions?
<--- Score

110. Were any designed experiments used to generate additional insight into the data analysis?
<--- Score

111. What are your Enterprise Technology processes?
<--- Score

112. What qualifications do Enterprise Technology

leaders need?
<--- Score

113. Do you, as a leader, bounce back quickly from setbacks?
<--- Score

114. What process improvements will be needed?
<--- Score

115. How do you ensure that the Enterprise Technology opportunity is realistic?
<--- Score

116. Have you defined which data is gathered how?
<--- Score

117. How do you promote understanding that opportunity for improvement is not criticism of the status quo, or the people who created the status quo?
<--- Score

118. What qualifications and skills do you need?
<--- Score

119. What data is gathered?
<--- Score

120. Is pre-qualification of suppliers carried out?
<--- Score

121. Where can you get qualified talent today?
<--- Score

122. How do mission and objectives affect the Enterprise Technology processes of your

organization?
<--- Score

123. What are the revised rough estimates of
the financial savings/opportunity for Enterprise
Technology improvements?
<--- Score

124. What do you need to qualify?
<--- Score

125. How do your work systems and key work
processes relate to and capitalize on your core
competencies?
<--- Score

126. What is the oversight process?
<--- Score

Add up total points for this section:
_ _ _ _ _ = Total points for this section

Divided by: _ _ _ _ _ _ (number of
statements answered) = _ _ _ _ _ _
Average score for this section

Transfer your score to the Enterprise
Technology Index at the beginning of
the Self-Assessment.

CRITERION #5: IMPROVE:

INTENT: Develop a practical solution. Innovate, establish and test the solution and to measure the results.

In my belief, the answer to this question is clearly defined:

5 Strongly Agree

4 Agree

3 Neutral

2 Disagree

1 Strongly Disagree

1. Have you identified breakpoints and/or risk tolerances that will trigger broad consideration of a potential need for intervention or modification of strategy?
<--- Score

2. How will the group know that the solution worked?
<--- Score

3. Who will be responsible for making the decisions to include or exclude requested changes once Enterprise Technology is underway?
<--- Score

4. What error proofing will be done to address some of the discrepancies observed in the 'as is' process?
<--- Score

5. What lessons, if any, from a pilot were incorporated into the design of the full-scale solution?
<--- Score

6. How are Enterprise Technology risks managed?
<--- Score

7. What were the underlying assumptions on the cost-benefit analysis?
<--- Score

8. How will you know that you have improved?
<--- Score

9. How are policy decisions made and where?
<--- Score

10. How do you improve Enterprise Technology service perception, and satisfaction?
<--- Score

11. If you could go back in time five years, what decision would you make differently? What is your best guess as to what decision you're making today you might regret five years from now?
<--- Score

12. For estimation problems, how do you develop an estimation statement?
<--- Score

13. What is the Enterprise Technology's sustainability risk?
<--- Score

14. What are the affordable Enterprise Technology risks?
<--- Score

15. At what point will vulnerability assessments be performed once Enterprise Technology is put into production (e.g., ongoing Risk Management after implementation)?
<--- Score

16. How do you link measurement and risk?
<--- Score

17. To what extent does management recognize Enterprise Technology as a tool to increase the results?
<--- Score

18. Do vendor agreements bring new compliance risk ?
<--- Score

19. How scalable is your Enterprise Technology solution?
<--- Score

20. What tools were used to evaluate the potential solutions?

<--- Score

21. What can you do to improve?
<--- Score

22. What is Enterprise Technology's impact on utilizing the best solution(s)?
<--- Score

23. Do you need to do a usability evaluation?
<--- Score

24. Are you assessing Enterprise Technology and risk?
<--- Score

25. What communications are necessary to support the implementation of the solution?
<--- Score

26. What criteria will you use to assess your Enterprise Technology risks?
<--- Score

27. How do you measure improved Enterprise Technology service perception, and satisfaction?
<--- Score

28. Is a contingency plan established?
<--- Score

29. Who will be using the results of the measurement activities?
<--- Score

30. How do you mitigate Enterprise Technology risk?
<--- Score

31. Who is in the roles of Chief Enterprise Architect, Enterprise Business Architect, Enterprise Information Architect, Enterprise Application/ Solution Architect, Enterprise Technology Architect?
<--- Score

32. What improvements have been achieved?
<--- Score

33. Is the optimal solution selected based on testing and analysis?
<--- Score

34. What were the criteria for evaluating a Enterprise Technology pilot?
<--- Score

35. What resources are required for the improvement efforts?
<--- Score

36. What actually has to improve and by how much?
<--- Score

37. Was a pilot designed for the proposed solution(s)?
<--- Score

38. Explorations of the frontiers of Enterprise Technology will help you build influence, improve Enterprise Technology, optimize decision making, and sustain change, what is your approach?
<--- Score

39. How does the solution remove the key sources of

issues discovered in the analyze phase?
<--- Score

40. How can skill-level changes improve Enterprise Technology?
<--- Score

41. What tools were used to tap into the creativity and encourage 'outside the box' thinking?
<--- Score

42. When you map the key players in your own work and the types/domains of relationships with them, which relationships do you find easy and which challenging, and why?
<--- Score

43. Is the measure of success for Enterprise Technology understandable to a variety of people?
<--- Score

44. What risks do you need to manage?
<--- Score

45. Is the solution technically practical?
<--- Score

46. Are there any constraints (technical, political, cultural, or otherwise) that would inhibit certain solutions?
<--- Score

47. How do you measure progress and evaluate training effectiveness?
<--- Score

48. How does your organization evaluate strategic Enterprise Technology success?
<--- Score

49. What practices helps your organization to develop its capacity to recognize patterns?
<--- Score

50. Do you cover the five essential competencies: Communication, Collaboration,Innovation, Adaptability, and Leadership that improve an organizations ability to leverage the new Enterprise Technology in a volatile global economy?
<--- Score

51. Is there a cost/benefit analysis of optimal solution(s)?
<--- Score

52. What strategies for Enterprise Technology improvement are successful?
<--- Score

53. What are your current levels and trends in key measures or indicators of workforce and leader development?
<--- Score

54. Who should make the Enterprise Technology decisions?
<--- Score

55. Who controls key decisions that will be made?
<--- Score

56. Who manages Enterprise Technology risk?

<--- Score

57. Risk events: what are the things that could go wrong?
<--- Score

58. Are events managed to resolution?
<--- Score

59. For decision problems, how do you develop a decision statement?
<--- Score

60. How can the phases of Enterprise Technology development be identified?
<--- Score

61. Are new and improved process ('should be') maps developed?
<--- Score

62. Was a Enterprise Technology charter developed?
<--- Score

63. How will the team or the process owner(s) monitor the implementation plan to see that it is working as intended?
<--- Score

64. Is the Enterprise Technology documentation thorough?
<--- Score

65. Does the goal represent a desired result that can be measured?
<--- Score

66. Are improved process ('should be') maps modified based on pilot data and analysis?
<--- Score

67. Is supporting Enterprise Technology documentation required?
<--- Score

68. In the past few months, what is the smallest change you have made that has had the biggest positive result? What was it about that small change that produced the large return?
<--- Score

69. How do you decide how much to remunerate an employee?
<--- Score

70. Is any Enterprise Technology documentation required?
<--- Score

71. What is the magnitude of the improvements?
<--- Score

72. What does the 'should be' process map/design look like?
<--- Score

73. Who do you report Enterprise Technology results to?
<--- Score

74. Can the solution be designed and implemented within an acceptable time period?

<--- Score

75. Are risk triggers captured?
<--- Score

76. How does the team improve its work?
<--- Score

77. How will you know that a change is an improvement?
<--- Score

78. Is the scope clearly documented?
<--- Score

79. How do you define the solutions' scope?
<--- Score

80. Which Enterprise Technology solution is appropriate?
<--- Score

81. Describe the design of the pilot and what tests were conducted, if any?
<--- Score

82. How will you measure the results?
<--- Score

83. Who makes the Enterprise Technology decisions in your organization?
<--- Score

84. What do you want to improve?
<--- Score

85. How significant is the improvement in the eyes of the end user?
<--- Score

86. Is the Enterprise Technology risk managed?
<--- Score

87. Why improve in the first place?
<--- Score

88. Are the best solutions selected?
<--- Score

89. Who are the key stakeholders for the Enterprise Technology evaluation?
<--- Score

90. How can you improve Enterprise Technology?
<--- Score

91. How do you keep improving Enterprise Technology?
<--- Score

92. Is pilot data collected and analyzed?
<--- Score

93. How do the Enterprise Technology results compare with the performance of your competitors and other organizations with similar offerings?
<--- Score

94. Do those selected for the Enterprise Technology team have a good general understanding of what Enterprise Technology is all about?
<--- Score

95. Have you achieved Enterprise Technology improvements?
<--- Score

96. Who controls the risk?
<--- Score

97. What are the concrete Enterprise Technology results?
<--- Score

98. Is there a high likelihood that any recommendations will achieve their intended results?
<--- Score

99. How do you improve productivity?
<--- Score

100. Can you identify any significant risks or exposures to Enterprise Technology third- parties (vendors, service providers, alliance partners etc) that concern you?
<--- Score

101. Is there a small-scale pilot for proposed improvement(s)? What conclusions were drawn from the outcomes of a pilot?
<--- Score

102. Is a solution implementation plan established, including schedule/work breakdown structure, resources, risk management plan, cost/budget, and control plan?
<--- Score

103. How did the team generate the list of possible solutions?
<--- Score

104. Were any criteria developed to assist the team in testing and evaluating potential solutions?
<--- Score

105. How risky is your organization?
<--- Score

106. Is risk periodically assessed?
<--- Score

107. Where do the Enterprise Technology decisions reside?
<--- Score

108. What to do with the results or outcomes of measurements?
<--- Score

109. What tools do you use once you have decided on a Enterprise Technology strategy and more importantly how do you choose?
<--- Score

110. What is the team's contingency plan for potential problems occurring in implementation?
<--- Score

111. How do you improve your likelihood of success ?
<--- Score

112. What Enterprise Technology improvements can be made?

<--- Score

113. Which of the recognised risks out of all risks can be most likely transferred?
<--- Score

114. Where do you need Enterprise Technology improvement?
<--- Score

115. What is the implementation plan?
<--- Score

116. Are decisions made in a timely manner?
<--- Score

117. Risk Identification: What are the possible risk events your organization faces in relation to Enterprise Technology?
<--- Score

118. Who are the people involved in developing and implementing Enterprise Technology?
<--- Score

119. What should a proof of concept or pilot accomplish?
<--- Score

120. Do you combine technical expertise with business knowledge and Enterprise Technology Key topics include lifecycles, development approaches, requirements and how to make a business case?
<--- Score

121. What tools were most useful during the improve

phase?

<--- Score

122. How do you manage and improve your Enterprise Technology work systems to deliver customer value and achieve organizational success and sustainability?

<--- Score

123. What is the risk?

<--- Score

124. What are the implications of the one critical Enterprise Technology decision 10 minutes, 10 months, and 10 years from now?

<--- Score

125. Will the controls trigger any other risks?

<--- Score

126. How can you better manage risk?

<--- Score

127. How do you manage Enterprise Technology risk?

<--- Score

128. How will you recognize and celebrate results?

<--- Score

129. What attendant changes will need to be made to ensure that the solution is successful?

<--- Score

130. Are possible solutions generated and tested?

<--- Score

131. Is the implementation plan designed?
<--- Score

132. How do you measure risk?
<--- Score

133. Who will be responsible for documenting the Enterprise Technology requirements in detail?
<--- Score

134. How do you deal with Enterprise Technology risk?
<--- Score

Add up total points for this section:
_ _ _ _ _ = Total points for this section

Divided by: _ _ _ _ _ _ (number of statements answered) = _ _ _ _ _ _
Average score for this section

Transfer your score to the Enterprise Technology Index at the beginning of the Self-Assessment.

CRITERION #6: CONTROL:

INTENT: Implement the practical solution. Maintain the performance and correct possible complications.

In my belief, the answer to this question is clearly defined:

5 Strongly Agree

4 Agree

3 Neutral

2 Disagree

1 Strongly Disagree

1. Is there a recommended audit plan for routine surveillance inspections of Enterprise Technology's gains?
<--- Score

2. Who controls critical resources?
<--- Score

3. How will Enterprise Technology decisions be made

and monitored?
<--- Score

4. How will the day-to-day responsibilities for monitoring and continual improvement be transferred from the improvement team to the process owner?
<--- Score

5. How can you best use all of your knowledge repositories to enhance learning and sharing?
<--- Score

6. What do your reports reflect?
<--- Score

7. Is knowledge gained on process shared and institutionalized?
<--- Score

8. Who has control over resources?
<--- Score

9. What are your results for key measures or indicators of the accomplishment of your Enterprise Technology strategy and action plans, including building and strengthening core competencies?
<--- Score

10. Who is the Enterprise Technology process owner?
<--- Score

11. Is the Enterprise Technology test/monitoring cost justified?
<--- Score

12. Will existing staff require re-training, for example, to learn new business processes?
<--- Score

13. How might the group capture best practices and lessons learned so as to leverage improvements?
<--- Score

14. Do you monitor the Enterprise Technology decisions made and fine tune them as they evolve?
<--- Score

15. What key inputs and outputs are being measured on an ongoing basis?
<--- Score

16. What is your plan to assess your security risks?
<--- Score

17. Do you monitor the effectiveness of your Enterprise Technology activities?
<--- Score

18. Does a troubleshooting guide exist or is it needed?
<--- Score

19. How do senior leaders actions reflect a commitment to the organizations Enterprise Technology values?
<--- Score

20. Are there documented procedures?
<--- Score

21. Does Enterprise Technology appropriately measure and monitor risk?

<--- Score

22. Is there a documented and implemented monitoring plan?
<--- Score

23. Against what alternative is success being measured?
<--- Score

24. Where do ideas that reach policy makers and planners as proposals for Enterprise Technology strengthening and reform actually originate?
<--- Score

25. Are you measuring, monitoring and predicting Enterprise Technology activities to optimize operations and profitability, and enhancing outcomes?
<--- Score

26. You may have created your quality measures at a time when you lacked resources, technology wasn't up to the required standard, or low service levels were the industry norm. Have those circumstances changed?
<--- Score

27. Are documented procedures clear and easy to follow for the operators?
<--- Score

28. Is a response plan established and deployed?
<--- Score

29. What are the key elements of your Enterprise

Technology performance improvement system, including your evaluation, organizational learning, and innovation processes?
<--- Score

30. What other systems, operations, processes, and infrastructures (hiring practices, staffing, training, incentives/rewards, metrics/dashboards/scorecards, etc.) need updates, additions, changes, or deletions in order to facilitate knowledge transfer and improvements?
<--- Score

31. What is the control/monitoring plan?
<--- Score

32. How do you select, collect, align, and integrate Enterprise Technology data and information for tracking daily operations and overall organizational performance, including progress relative to strategic objectives and action plans?
<--- Score

33. What other areas of the group might benefit from the Enterprise Technology team's improvements, knowledge, and learning?
<--- Score

34. What is your theory of human motivation, and how does your compensation plan fit with that view?
<--- Score

35. How do you plan for the cost of succession?
<--- Score

36. Does job training on the documented procedures

need to be part of the process team's education and
training?
<--- Score

37. Can support from partners be adjusted?
<--- Score

38. Are the planned controls working?
<--- Score

39. Is there a control plan in place for sustaining
improvements (short and long-term)?
<--- Score

40. How will report readings be checked to effectively
monitor performance?
<--- Score

41. Are suggested corrective/restorative actions
indicated on the response plan for known causes to
problems that might surface?
<--- Score

42. What should you measure to verify efficiency
gains?
<--- Score

43. How will new or emerging customer needs/
requirements be checked/communicated to orient
the process toward meeting the new specifications
and continually reducing variation?
<--- Score

44. Are the Enterprise Technology standards
challenging?
<--- Score

45. What is the best design framework for Enterprise Technology organization now that, in a post industrial-age if the top-down, command and control model is no longer relevant?
<--- Score

46. Do the Enterprise Technology decisions you make today help people and the planet tomorrow?
<--- Score

47. How will the process owner and team be able to hold the gains?
<--- Score

48. What do you stand for--and what are you against?
<--- Score

49. What should the next improvement project be that is related to Enterprise Technology?
<--- Score

50. Is a response plan in place for when the input, process, or output measures indicate an 'out-of-control' condition?
<--- Score

51. Are new process steps, standards, and documentation ingrained into normal operations?
<--- Score

52. How do you spread information?
<--- Score

53. How do you monitor usage and cost?
<--- Score

54. How will you measure your QA plan's effectiveness?
<--- Score

55. How likely is the current Enterprise Technology plan to come in on schedule or on budget?
<--- Score

56. Does the response plan contain a definite closed loop continual improvement scheme (e.g., plan-do-check-act)?
<--- Score

57. What do you measure to verify effectiveness gains?
<--- Score

58. Who is going to spread your message?
<--- Score

59. How do your controls stack up?
<--- Score

60. What are customers monitoring?
<--- Score

61. Does the Enterprise Technology performance meet the customer's requirements?
<--- Score

62. What can you control?
<--- Score

63. What are you attempting to measure/monitor?
<--- Score

64. Will the team be available to assist members in planning investigations?
<--- Score

65. How is change control managed?
<--- Score

66. Can you adapt and adjust to changing Enterprise Technology situations?
<--- Score

67. How do you plan on providing proper recognition and disclosure of supporting companies?
<--- Score

68. How do controls support value?
<--- Score

69. What Enterprise Technology standards are applicable?
<--- Score

70. Has the improved process and its steps been standardized?
<--- Score

71. What are the known security controls?
<--- Score

72. How widespread is its use?
<--- Score

73. How do you establish and deploy modified action plans if circumstances require a shift in plans and rapid execution of new plans?

<--- Score

74. Is reporting being used or needed?
<--- Score

75. Who sets the Enterprise Technology standards?
<--- Score

76. How will the process owner verify improvement in present and future sigma levels, process capabilities?
<--- Score

77. Are controls in place and consistently applied?
<--- Score

78. Is there a Enterprise Technology Communication plan covering who needs to get what information when?
<--- Score

79. What quality tools were useful in the control phase?
<--- Score

80. Is there an action plan in case of emergencies?
<--- Score

81. Who will be in control?
<--- Score

82. Is there a standardized process?
<--- Score

83. Will your goals reflect your program budget?
<--- Score

84. How do you encourage people to take control and responsibility?
<--- Score

85. How will input, process, and output variables be checked to detect for sub-optimal conditions?
<--- Score

86. What are the critical parameters to watch?
<--- Score

87. Is there a transfer of ownership and knowledge to process owner and process team tasked with the responsibilities.
<--- Score

88. Implementation Planning: is a pilot needed to test the changes before a full roll out occurs?
<--- Score

89. Is there documentation that will support the successful operation of the improvement?
<--- Score

90. Are pertinent alerts monitored, analyzed and distributed to appropriate personnel?
<--- Score

91. Are operating procedures consistent?
<--- Score

92. How is Enterprise Technology project cost planned, managed, monitored?
<--- Score

93. Have new or revised work instructions resulted?

<--- Score

94. In the case of a Enterprise Technology project, the criteria for the audit derive from implementation objectives, an audit of a Enterprise Technology project involves assessing whether the recommendations outlined for implementation have been met, can you track that any Enterprise Technology project is implemented as planned, and is it working?
<--- Score

95. Will any special training be provided for results interpretation?
<--- Score

96. What is the recommended frequency of auditing?
<--- Score

97. Is new knowledge gained imbedded in the response plan?
<--- Score

Add up total points for this section:
_____ = Total points for this section

Divided by: _____ (number of statements answered) = _____
Average score for this section

Transfer your score to the Enterprise Technology Index at the beginning of the Self-Assessment.

CRITERION #7: SUSTAIN:

INTENT: Retain the benefits.

In my belief, the answer to this question is clearly defined:

5 Strongly Agree

4 Agree

3 Neutral

2 Disagree

1 Strongly Disagree

1. What would you recommend your friend do if he/she were facing this dilemma?
<--- Score

2. What are the long-term Enterprise Technology goals?
<--- Score

3. In retrospect, of the projects that you pulled the plug on, what percent do you wish had been allowed to keep going, and what percent do you wish had

ended earlier?
<--- Score

4. In a project to restructure Enterprise Technology outcomes, which stakeholders would you involve?
<--- Score

5. What is the kind of project structure that would be appropriate for your Enterprise Technology project, should it be formal and complex, or can it be less formal and relatively simple?
<--- Score

6. Which Enterprise Technology goals are the most important?
<--- Score

7. What are the performance and scale of the Enterprise Technology tools?
<--- Score

8. Can you break it down?
<--- Score

9. If you had to leave your organization for a year and the only communication you could have with employees/colleagues was a single paragraph, what would you write?
<--- Score

10. Who do we want your customers to become?
<--- Score

11. What you are going to do to affect the numbers?
<--- Score

12. How is implementation research currently incorporated into each of your goals?
<--- Score

13. What is it like to work for you?
<--- Score

14. Will it be accepted by users?
<--- Score

15. How do you determine the key elements that affect Enterprise Technology workforce satisfaction, how are these elements determined for different workforce groups and segments?
<--- Score

16. Will there be any necessary staff changes (redundancies or new hires)?
<--- Score

17. What will be the consequences to the stakeholder (financial, reputation etc) if Enterprise Technology does not go ahead or fails to deliver the objectives?
<--- Score

18. Who is responsible for Enterprise Technology?
<--- Score

19. What do we do when new problems arise?
<--- Score

20. Who will be responsible for deciding whether Enterprise Technology goes ahead or not after the initial investigations?
<--- Score

21. If your customer were your grandmother, would you tell her to buy what you're selling?
<--- Score

22. Do you have enough freaky customers in your portfolio pushing you to the limit day in and day out?
<--- Score

23. How do you engage the workforce, in addition to satisfying them?
<--- Score

24. Who, on the executive team or the board, has spoken to a customer recently?
<--- Score

25. How do you maintain Enterprise Technology's Integrity?
<--- Score

26. What trouble can you get into?
<--- Score

27. If your company went out of business tomorrow, would anyone who doesn't get a paycheck here care?
<--- Score

28. Is a Enterprise Technology team work effort in place?
<--- Score

29. Who do you want your customers to become?
<--- Score

30. Are your responses positive or negative?
<--- Score

31. What are your most important goals for the strategic Enterprise Technology objectives?
<--- Score

32. Who are the key stakeholders?
<--- Score

33. Who is responsible for ensuring appropriate resources (time, people and money) are allocated to Enterprise Technology?
<--- Score

34. Do you think you know, or do you know you know ?
<--- Score

35. Which individuals, teams or departments will be involved in Enterprise Technology?
<--- Score

36. Is a Enterprise Technology breakthrough on the horizon?
<--- Score

37. What would have to be true for the option on the table to be the best possible choice?
<--- Score

38. Is Enterprise Technology dependent on the successful delivery of a current project?
<--- Score

39. Were lessons learned captured and communicated?
<--- Score

40. If you had to rebuild your organization without any traditional competitive advantages (i.e., no killer technology, promising research, innovative product/ service delivery model, etcetera), how would your people have to approach their work and collaborate together in order to create the necessary conditions for success?
<--- Score

41. What are the essentials of internal Enterprise Technology management?
<--- Score

42. Are you / should you be revolutionary or evolutionary?
<--- Score

43. What business benefits will Enterprise Technology goals deliver if achieved?
<--- Score

44. Do you have past Enterprise Technology successes?
<--- Score

45. What are you trying to prove to yourself, and how might it be hijacking your life and business success?
<--- Score

46. Who else should you help?
<--- Score

47. Why do and why don't your customers like your organization?
<--- Score

48. Do you feel that more should be done in the Enterprise Technology area?
<--- Score

49. If you do not follow, then how to lead?
<--- Score

50. What unique value proposition (UVP) do you offer?
<--- Score

51. Who are your customers?
<--- Score

52. How do you provide a safe environment -physically and emotionally?
<--- Score

53. Who will determine interim and final deadlines?
<--- Score

54. What management system can you use to leverage the Enterprise Technology experience, ideas, and concerns of the people closest to the work to be done?
<--- Score

55. What one word do you want to own in the minds of your customers, employees, and partners?
<--- Score

56. Who will provide the final approval of Enterprise Technology deliverables?
<--- Score

57. How important is Enterprise Technology to the

user organizations mission?
<--- Score

58. What are internal and external Enterprise Technology relations?
<--- Score

59. What could happen if you do not do it?
<--- Score

60. What are your personal philosophies regarding Enterprise Technology and how do they influence your work?
<--- Score

61. Whom among your colleagues do you trust, and for what?
<--- Score

62. Are you paying enough attention to the partners your company depends on to succeed?
<--- Score

63. Why is it important to have senior management support for a Enterprise Technology project?
<--- Score

64. Why not do Enterprise Technology?
<--- Score

65. Instead of going to current contacts for new ideas, what if you reconnected with dormant contacts-- the people you used to know? If you were going reactivate a dormant tie, who would it be?
<--- Score

66. Are the criteria for selecting recommendations stated?
<--- Score

67. What goals did you miss?
<--- Score

68. What are strategies for increasing support and reducing opposition?
<--- Score

69. What is your BATNA (best alternative to a negotiated agreement)?
<--- Score

70. How do you manage Enterprise Technology Knowledge Management (KM)?
<--- Score

71. Why is Enterprise Technology important for you now?
<--- Score

72. What happens when a new employee joins the organization?
<--- Score

73. Ask yourself: how would you do this work if you only had one staff member to do it?
<--- Score

74. What information is critical to your organization that your executives are ignoring?
<--- Score

75. Have new benefits been realized?

<--- Score

76. Are you maintaining a past–present–future perspective throughout the Enterprise Technology discussion?
<--- Score

77. Do Enterprise Technology rules make a reasonable demand on a users capabilities?
<--- Score

78. What are the usability implications of Enterprise Technology actions?
<--- Score

79. Why should people listen to you?
<--- Score

80. If you find that you havent accomplished one of the goals for one of the steps of the Enterprise Technology strategy, what will you do to fix it?
<--- Score

81. How do you ensure that implementations of Enterprise Technology products are done in a way that ensures safety?
<--- Score

82. Is your basic point _____ or _____?
<--- Score

83. Is your strategy driving your strategy? Or is the way in which you allocate resources driving your strategy?
<--- Score

84. How do you foster innovation?
<--- Score

85. How can you become the company that would put you out of business?
<--- Score

86. Is it economical; do you have the time and money?
<--- Score

87. What new services of functionality will be implemented next with Enterprise Technology ?
<--- Score

88. How do you keep records, of what?
<--- Score

89. What role does communication play in the success or failure of a Enterprise Technology project?
<--- Score

90. Are you satisfied with your current role? If not, what is missing from it?
<--- Score

91. What knowledge, skills and characteristics mark a good Enterprise Technology project manager?
<--- Score

92. How likely is it that a customer would recommend your company to a friend or colleague?
<--- Score

93. What must you excel at?
<--- Score

94. What is effective Enterprise Technology?
<--- Score

95. What is the funding source for this project?
<--- Score

96. What counts that you are not counting?
<--- Score

97. Are there any activities that you can take off your to do list?
<--- Score

98. What does your signature ensure?
<--- Score

99. Whose voice (department, ethnic group, women, older workers, etc) might you have missed hearing from in your company, and how might you amplify this voice to create positive momentum for your business?
<--- Score

100. What stupid rule would you most like to kill?
<--- Score

101. If you were responsible for initiating and implementing major changes in your organization, what steps might you take to ensure acceptance of those changes?
<--- Score

102. Have benefits been optimized with all key stakeholders?
<--- Score

103. Do you think Enterprise Technology accomplishes the goals you expect it to accomplish?
<--- Score

104. How much does Enterprise Technology help?
<--- Score

105. Why should you adopt a Enterprise Technology framework?
<--- Score

106. How do you make it meaningful in connecting Enterprise Technology with what users do day-to-day?
<--- Score

107. Think of your Enterprise Technology project, what are the main functions?
<--- Score

108. How do you go about securing Enterprise Technology?
<--- Score

109. Who is on the team?
<--- Score

110. How are you doing compared to your industry?
<--- Score

111. Who are four people whose careers you have enhanced?
<--- Score

112. What was the last experiment you ran?
<--- Score

113. How do you govern and fulfill your societal responsibilities?
<--- Score

114. What are the top 3 things at the forefront of your Enterprise Technology agendas for the next 3 years?
<--- Score

115. What relationships among Enterprise Technology trends do you perceive?
<--- Score

116. How do you proactively clarify deliverables and Enterprise Technology quality expectations?
<--- Score

117. What is the overall talent health of your organization as a whole at senior levels, and for each organization reporting to a member of the Senior Leadership Team?
<--- Score

118. What did you miss in the interview for the worst hire you ever made?
<--- Score

119. Is the Enterprise Technology organization completing tasks effectively and efficiently?
<--- Score

120. What are the business goals Enterprise Technology is aiming to achieve?
<--- Score

121. How do you keep the momentum going?
<--- Score

122. Do you know who is a friend or a foe?
<--- Score

123. How will you insure seamless interoperability of Enterprise Technology moving forward?
<--- Score

124. Are the assumptions believable and achievable?
<--- Score

125. Operational - will it work?
<--- Score

126. What is the overall business strategy?
<--- Score

127. If no one would ever find out about your accomplishments, how would you lead differently?
<--- Score

128. What are specific Enterprise Technology rules to follow?
<--- Score

129. How do you accomplish your long range Enterprise Technology goals?
<--- Score

130. What threat is Enterprise Technology addressing?
<--- Score

131. Which models, tools and techniques are necessary?
<--- Score

132. How do you foster the skills, knowledge, talents, attributes, and characteristics you want to have?
<--- Score

133. Where can you break convention?
<--- Score

134. How much contingency will be available in the budget?
<--- Score

135. How do you create buy-in?
<--- Score

136. How do you assess the Enterprise Technology pitfalls that are inherent in implementing it?
<--- Score

137. What is the craziest thing you can do?
<--- Score

138. What are the challenges?
<--- Score

139. How do you listen to customers to obtain actionable information?
<--- Score

140. What is the purpose of Enterprise Technology in relation to the mission?
<--- Score

141. To whom do you add value?
<--- Score

142. What is your competitive advantage?

<--- Score

143. What happens at your organization when people fail?
<--- Score

144. What is the range of capabilities?
<--- Score

145. Is the impact that Enterprise Technology has shown?
<--- Score

146. What Enterprise Technology skills are most important?
<--- Score

147. How does Enterprise Technology integrate with other stakeholder initiatives?
<--- Score

148. How will you know that the Enterprise Technology project has been successful?
<--- Score

149. Is there any reason to believe the opposite of my current belief?
<--- Score

150. Do you say no to customers for no reason?
<--- Score

151. Do you see more potential in people than they do in themselves?
<--- Score

152. What is the big Enterprise Technology idea?
<--- Score

153. How do you transition from the baseline to the target?
<--- Score

154. What have you done to protect your business from competitive encroachment?
<--- Score

155. What are the key enablers to make this Enterprise Technology move?
<--- Score

156. Are assumptions made in Enterprise Technology stated explicitly?
<--- Score

157. Political -is anyone trying to undermine this project?
<--- Score

158. How do senior leaders deploy your organizations vision and values through your leadership system, to the workforce, to key suppliers and partners, and to customers and other stakeholders, as appropriate?
<--- Score

159. How will you motivate the stakeholders with the least vested interest?
<--- Score

160. Do you have the right people on the bus?
<--- Score

161. What are the potential basics of Enterprise Technology fraud?
<--- Score

162. What is your Enterprise Technology strategy?
<--- Score

163. If you got fired and a new hire took your place, what would she do different?
<--- Score

164. Marketing budgets are tighter, consumers are more skeptical, and social media has changed forever the way we talk about Enterprise Technology, how do you gain traction?
<--- Score

165. Can the schedule be done in the given time?
<--- Score

166. How will you ensure you get what you expected?
<--- Score

167. What are the barriers to increased Enterprise Technology production?
<--- Score

168. How do you stay inspired?
<--- Score

169. Can you do all this work?
<--- Score

170. In the past year, what have you done (or could you have done) to increase the accurate perception of your company/brand as ethical and honest?

<--- Score

171. How can you become more high-tech but still be high touch?
<--- Score

172. Did your employees make progress today?
<--- Score

173. Has implementation been effective in reaching specified objectives so far?
<--- Score

174. Is maximizing Enterprise Technology protection the same as minimizing Enterprise Technology loss?
<--- Score

175. How do you track customer value, profitability or financial return, organizational success, and sustainability?
<--- Score

176. Are you changing as fast as the world around you?
<--- Score

177. What are the rules and assumptions your industry operates under? What if the opposite were true?
<--- Score

178. Are you relevant? Will you be relevant five years from now? Ten?
<--- Score

179. What are current Enterprise Technology paradigms?

<--- Score

180. When information truly is ubiquitous, when reach and connectivity are completely global, when computing resources are infinite, and when a whole new set of impossibilities are not only possible, but happening, what will that do to your business?
<--- Score

181. What is your question? Why?
<--- Score

182. Who do you think the world wants your organization to be?
<--- Score

183. What potential megatrends could make your business model obsolete?
<--- Score

184. What is the recommended frequency of auditing?
<--- Score

185. If there were zero limitations, what would you do differently?
<--- Score

186. Would you rather sell to knowledgeable and informed customers or to uninformed customers?
<--- Score

187. How long will it take to change?
<--- Score

188. What is the estimated value of the project?
<--- Score

189. What current systems have to be understood and/or changed?
<--- Score

190. What trophy do you want on your mantle?
<--- Score

191. Is there a work around that you can use?
<--- Score

192. How do you set Enterprise Technology stretch targets and how do you get people to not only participate in setting these stretch targets but also that they strive to achieve these?
<--- Score

193. What are the short and long-term Enterprise Technology goals?
<--- Score

194. At what moment would you think; Will I get fired?
<--- Score

195. What is the source of the strategies for Enterprise Technology strengthening and reform?
<--- Score

196. How do you know if you are successful?
<--- Score

197. Do you have an implicit bias for capital investments over people investments?
<--- Score

198. What should you stop doing?

<--- Score

199. Is there any existing Enterprise Technology governance structure?
<--- Score

200. What may be the consequences for the performance of an organization if all stakeholders are not consulted regarding Enterprise Technology?
<--- Score

201. How do you deal with Enterprise Technology changes?
<--- Score

202. How can you negotiate Enterprise Technology successfully with a stubborn boss, an irate client, or a deceitful coworker?
<--- Score

203. Who is the main stakeholder, with ultimate responsibility for driving Enterprise Technology forward?
<--- Score

204. What are the success criteria that will indicate that Enterprise Technology objectives have been met and the benefits delivered?
<--- Score

205. Who is responsible for errors?
<--- Score

206. What happens if you do not have enough funding?
<--- Score

207. What Enterprise Technology modifications can you make work for you?
<--- Score

208. What is your formula for success in Enterprise Technology ?
<--- Score

209. Are you using a design thinking approach and integrating Innovation, Enterprise Technology Experience, and Brand Value?
<--- Score

210. What are you challenging?
<--- Score

211. What have been your experiences in defining long range Enterprise Technology goals?
<--- Score

212. Why will customers want to buy your organizations products/services?
<--- Score

213. If you weren't already in this business, would you enter it today? And if not, what are you going to do about it?
<--- Score

214. Are new benefits received and understood?
<--- Score

Add up total points for this section:
_ _ _ _ _ = Total points for this section

Divided by: _____ (number of
statements answered) = _____
Average score for this section

Transfer your score to the Enterprise
Technology Index at the beginning of
the Self-Assessment.

Enterprise Technology and Managing Projects, Criteria for Project Managers:

1.0 Initiating Process Group: Enterprise Technology

1. Are you just doing busywork to pass the time?

2. Are you properly tracking the progress of the Enterprise Technology project and communicating the status to stakeholders?

3. What are the constraints?

4. How do you help others satisfy needs?

5. At which stage, in a typical Enterprise Technology project do stake holders have maximum influence?

6. What technical work to do in each phase?

7. Do you know the roles & responsibilities required for this Enterprise Technology project?

8. What are the tools and techniques to be used in each phase?

9. Did the Enterprise Technology project team have the right skills?

10. What are the inputs required to produce the deliverables?

11. What business situation is being addressed?

12. Which of six sigmas dmaic phases focuses on the measurement of internal process that affect factors that are critical to quality?

13. Have the stakeholders identified all individual requirements pertaining to business process?

14. What do you need to do?

15. When must it be done?

16. First of all, should any action be taken?

17. Although the Enterprise Technology project manager does not directly manage procurement and contracting activities, who does manage procurement and contracting activities in your organization then if not the PM?

18. What were things that you did very well and want to do the same again on the next Enterprise Technology project?

19. Do you know all the stakeholders impacted by the Enterprise Technology project and what needs are?

20. How well defined and documented were the Enterprise Technology project management processes you chose to use?

1.1 Project Charter: Enterprise Technology

21. Where and how does the team fit within your organization structure?

22. What is the most common tool for helping define the detail?

23. Fit with other Products Compliments – Cannibalizes?

24. Environmental stewardship and sustainability considerations: what is the process that will be used to ensure compliance with the environmental stewardship policy?

25. What are the known stakeholder requirements?

26. Who is the Enterprise Technology project Manager?

27. Are you building in-house ?

28. Why have you chosen the aim you have set forth?

29. Did your Enterprise Technology project ask for this?

30. Why Outsource?

31. Why is a Enterprise Technology project Charter used?

32. When do you use a Enterprise Technology project Charter?

33. Customer benefits: what customer requirements does this Enterprise Technology project address?

34. What barriers do you predict to your success?

35. Why use a Enterprise Technology project charter?

36. What is in it for you?

37. Avoid costs, improve service, and/ or comply with a mandate?

38. Who will take notes, document decisions?

1.2 Stakeholder Register: Enterprise Technology

39. Is your organization ready for change?

40. How should employers make voices heard?

41. How big is the gap?

42. What opportunities exist to provide communications?

43. Who are the stakeholders?

44. What is the power of the stakeholder?

45. Who is managing stakeholder engagement?

46. How will reports be created?

47. What are the major Enterprise Technology project milestones requiring communications or providing communications opportunities?

48. What & Why?

49. Who wants to talk about Security?

50. How much influence do they have on the Enterprise Technology project?

1.3 Stakeholder Analysis Matrix: Enterprise Technology

51. Contributions to policy and practice?

52. Are there people who ise voices or interests in the issue may not be heard?

53. How to involve media?

54. Why do you need to manage Enterprise Technology project Risk?

55. Financial reserves, likely returns?

56. What resources might the stakeholder bring to the Enterprise Technology project?

57. Guiding question: who shall you involve in the making of the stakeholder map?

58. Own known vulnerabilities?

59. Information and research?

60. What tools would help you communicate?

61. Management cover, succession?

62. How to measure the achievement of the Outputs?

63. Usps (unique selling points)?

64. Processes and systems, etc?

65. How will the stakeholder directly benefit from the Enterprise Technology project and how will this affect the stakeholders motivation?

66. Continuity, supply chain robustness?

67. Inoculations or payment to receive them?

68. Who has not been involved up to now and should have been?

69. How to measure the achievement of the Immediate Objective?

70. Geographical, export, import?

2.0 Planning Process Group: Enterprise Technology

71. Explanation: is what the Enterprise Technology project intents to solve a hard question?

72. Are work methodologies, financial instruments, etc. shared among departments, organizations and Enterprise Technology projects?

73. Is the identification of the problems, inequalities and gaps, with respective causes, clear in the Enterprise Technology project?

74. Professionals want to know what is expected from them; what are the deliverables?

75. To what extent and in what ways are the Enterprise Technology project contributing to progress towards organizational reform?

76. Just how important is your work to the overall success of the Enterprise Technology project?

77. To what extent have public/private national resources and/or counterparts been mobilized to contribute to the programs objective and produce results and impacts?

78. In what ways can the governance of the Enterprise Technology project be improved so that it has greater likelihood of achieving future sustainability?

79. How can you tell when you are done?

80. What makes your Enterprise Technology project successful?

81. In what way has the program contributed towards the issue culture and development included on the public agenda?

82. Who are the Enterprise Technology project stakeholders?

83. You are creating your WBS and find that you keep decomposing tasks into smaller and smaller units. How can you tell when you are done?

84. How does activity resource estimation affect activity duration estimation?

85. How well defined and documented are the Enterprise Technology project management processes you chose to use?

86. Are the follow-up indicators relevant and do they meet the quality needed to measure the outputs and outcomes of the Enterprise Technology project?

87. Contingency planning. if a risk event occurs, what will you do?

88. What will you do to minimize the impact should a risk event occur?

89. What is the difference between the early schedule and late schedule?

90. How should needs be met?

2.1 Project Management Plan: Enterprise Technology

91. What are the assumptions?

92. What is risk management?

93. What is Enterprise Technology project scope management?

94. How well are you able to manage your risk?

95. What should you drop in order to add something new?

96. What are the assigned resources?

97. How can you best help your organization to develop consistent practices in Enterprise Technology project management planning stages?

98. Are comparable cost estimates used for comparing, screening and selecting alternative plans, and has a reasonable cost estimate been developed for the recommended plan?

99. If the Enterprise Technology project is complex or scope is specialized, do you have appropriate and/or qualified staff available to perform the tasks?

100. Are the existing and future without-plan conditions reasonable and appropriate?

101. Are there non-structural buyout or relocation recommendations?

102. Is there anything you would now do differently on your Enterprise Technology project based on past experience?

103. What is the justification?

104. Who manages integration?

105. Is the budget realistic?

106. Are calculations and results of analyzes essentially correct?

107. Do there need to be organizational changes?

108. Does the implementation plan have an appropriate division of responsibilities?

109. Is the appropriate plan selected based on your organizations objectives and evaluation criteria expressed in Principles and Guidelines policies?

2.2 Scope Management Plan: Enterprise Technology

110. Time estimation – how much time will be needed?

111. Have all documents been archived in a Enterprise Technology project repository for each release?

112. Has a Enterprise Technology project Communications Plan been developed?

113. Are you doing what you have set out to do?

114. Has a provision been made to reassess Enterprise Technology project risks at various Enterprise Technology project stages?

115. Are written status reports provided on a designated frequent basis?

116. Have the key functions and capabilities been defined and assigned to each release or iteration?

117. Has a sponsor been identified?

118. Will anyone else be involved in verifying the deliverables?

119. Are alternatives safe, functional, constructible, economical, reasonable and sustainable?

120. Are cause and effect determined for risks when

they occur?

121. Have Enterprise Technology project team accountabilities & responsibilities been clearly defined?

122. Have the personnel with the necessary skills and competence been identified and has agreement for participation in the Enterprise Technology project been reached with the appropriate management?

123. Is it possible to track all classes of Enterprise Technology project work (e.g. scheduled, un-scheduled, defect repair, etc.)?

124. Have external dependencies been captured in the schedule?

125. Can each item be appropriately scheduled?

126. Is there a scope management plan that includes how Enterprise Technology project scope will be defined, developed, monitored, validated and controlled?

127. Has a structured approach been used to break work effort into manageable components (WBS)?

128. Are measurements and feedback mechanisms incorporated in tracking work effort & refining work estimating techniques?

2.3 Requirements Management Plan: Enterprise Technology

129. Do you know which stakeholders will participate in the requirements effort?

130. Will the contractors involved take full responsibility?

131. Does the Enterprise Technology project have a Change Control process?

132. The wbs is developed as part of a joint planning session. and how do you know that youhave done this right?

133. Is the system software (non-operating system) new to the IT Enterprise Technology project team?

134. How often will the reporting occur?

135. Is it new or replacing an existing business system or process?

136. Did you provide clear and concise specifications?

137. How will the requirements become prioritized?

138. Define the help desk model. who will take full responsibility?

139. Do you have price sheets and a methodology for determining the total proposal cost?

140. Are actual resource expenditures versus planned still acceptable?

141. Business analysis scope?

142. In case of software development; Should you have a test for each code module?

143. To see if a requirement statement is sufficiently well-defined, read it from the developers perspective. Mentally add the phrase, call me when youre done to the end of the requirement and see if that makes you nervous. In other words, would you need additional clarification from the author to understand the requirement well enough to design and implement it?

144. When and how will a requirements baseline be established in this Enterprise Technology project?

145. Are all the stakeholders ready for the transition into the user community?

146. Subject to change control?

147. Why manage requirements?

148. If it exists, where is it housed?

2.4 Requirements Documentation: Enterprise Technology

149. Completeness. are all functions required by the customer included?

150. Are there any requirements conflicts?

151. What variations exist for a process?

152. How much testing do you need to do to prove that your system is safe?

153. What images does it conjure?

154. How linear / iterative is your Requirements Gathering process (or will it be)?

155. What is a show stopper in the requirements?

156. Where do you define what is a customer, what are the attributes of customer?

157. Who is involved?

158. How will they be documented / shared?

159. What kind of entity is a problem ?

160. What are the potential disadvantages/ advantages?

161. Can you check system requirements?

162. How to document system requirements?

163. What will be the integration problems?

164. Have the benefits identified with the system being identified clearly?

165. How does what is being described meet the business need?

166. Who is interacting with the system?

167. Is the requirement realistically testable?

2.5 Requirements Traceability Matrix: Enterprise Technology

168. What is the WBS?

169. Will you use a Requirements Traceability Matrix?

170. Is there a requirements traceability process in place?

171. Describe the process for approving requirements so they can be added to the traceability matrix and Enterprise Technology project work can be performed. Will the Enterprise Technology project requirements become approved in writing?

172. Why use a WBS?

173. What percentage of Enterprise Technology projects are producing traceability matrices between requirements and other work products?

174. Do you have a clear understanding of all subcontracts in place?

175. How do you manage scope?

176. How will it affect the stakeholders personally in career?

177. Why do you manage scope?

178. What are the chronologies, contingencies,

consequences, criteria?

179. How small is small enough?

2.6 Project Scope Statement: Enterprise Technology

180. Which risks does the Enterprise Technology project focus on?

181. What are the major deliverables of the Enterprise Technology project?

182. Is this process communicated to the customer and team members?

183. Is the quality function identified and assigned?

184. If there is an independent oversight contractor, have they signed off on the Enterprise Technology project Plan?

185. Elements that deal with providing the detail?

186. Any new risks introduced or old risks impacted. Are there issues that could affect the existing requirements for the result, service, or product if the scope changes?

187. Has a method and process for requirement tracking been developed?

188. Does the scope statement still need some clarity?

189. Did your Enterprise Technology project ask for this?

190. How often do you estimate that the scope might change, and why?

191. Have the configuration management functions been assigned?

192. Once its defined, what is the stability of the Enterprise Technology project scope?

193. What process would you recommend for creating the Enterprise Technology project scope statement?

194. Have you been able to easily identify success criteria and create objective measurements for each of the Enterprise Technology project scopes goal statements?

195. Elements of scope management that deal with concept development ?

196. Change management vs. change leadership - what is the difference?

197. Are the input requirements from the team members clearly documented and communicated?

2.7 Assumption and Constraint Log: Enterprise Technology

198. Are there procedures in place to effectively manage interdependencies with other Enterprise Technology projects / systems?

199. Is the process working, and people are not executing in compliance of the process?

200. Are there processes in place to ensure that all the terms and code concepts have been documented consistently?

201. Have all necessary approvals been obtained?

202. No superfluous information or marketing narrative?

203. Have all involved stakeholders and work groups committed to the Enterprise Technology project?

204. Have Enterprise Technology project management standards and procedures been established and documented?

205. What weaknesses do you have?

206. What is positive about the current process?

207. Violation trace: why ?

208. Have the scope, objectives, costs, benefits and

impacts been communicated to all involved and/or impacted stakeholders and work groups?

209. Does the traceability documentation describe the tool and/or mechanism to be used to capture traceability throughout the life cycle?

210. What would you gain if you spent time working to improve this process?

211. Are funding and staffing resource estimates sufficiently detailed and documented for use in planning and tracking the Enterprise Technology project?

212. Are there processes defining how software will be developed including development methods, overall timeline for development, software product standards, and traceability?

213. Have you eliminated all duplicative tasks or manual efforts, where appropriate?

214. Can the requirements be traced to the appropriate components of the solution, as well as test scripts?

215. Does the system design reflect the requirements?

216. Is this model reasonable?

217. Are requirements management tracking tools and procedures in place?

2.8 Work Breakdown Structure: Enterprise Technology

218. Why is it useful?

219. How much detail?

220. When would you develop a Work Breakdown Structure?

221. Is it a change in scope?

222. Can you make it?

223. Where does it take place?

224. How will you and your Enterprise Technology project team define the Enterprise Technology projects scope and work breakdown structure?

225. How big is a work-package?

226. What is the probability of completing the Enterprise Technology project in less that xx days?

227. What has to be done?

228. What is the probability that the Enterprise Technology project duration will exceed xx weeks?

229. Is it still viable?

230. Who has to do it?

231. When do you stop?

232. Why would you develop a Work Breakdown Structure?

233. When does it have to be done?

2.9 WBS Dictionary: Enterprise Technology

234. Is the work done on a work package level as described in the WBS dictionary?

235. Is cost performance measurement at the point in time most suitable for the category of material involved, and no earlier than the time of actual receipt of material?

236. Software specification, development, integration, and testing, licenses ?

237. Do work packages consist of discrete tasks which are adequately described?

238. Is the entire contract planned in time-phased control accounts to the extent practicable?

239. Are work packages assigned to performing organizations?

240. How detailed should a Enterprise Technology project get?

241. Can the contractor substantiate work package and planning package budgets?

242. Are the bases and rates for allocating costs from each indirect pool consistently applied?

243. Changes in the overhead pool and/or

organization structures?

244. Are the overhead pools formally and adequately identified?

245. Are the contractors estimates of costs at completion reconcilable with cost data reported to us?

246. Are work packages reasonably short in time duration or do they have adequate objective indicators/milestones to minimize subjectivity of the in process work evaluation?

247. Authorization to proceed with all authorized work?

248. Does the contractors system include procedures for measuring the performance of critical subcontractors?

249. Are overhead costs budgets established on a basis consistent with anticipated direct business base?

250. Do you need another level?

251. Is all contract work included in the CWBS?

252. Are all elements of indirect expense identified to overhead cost budgets of Enterprise Technology projections?

253. Actual cost of work performed?

2.10 Schedule Management Plan: Enterprise Technology

254. What will be the final cost of the Enterprise Technology project if status quo is maintained?

255. Who is responsible for estimating the activity resources?

256. List all schedule constraints here. Must the Enterprise Technology project be complete by a specified date?

257. Is there a formal set of procedures supporting Stakeholder Management?

258. Are there checklists created to determine if all quality processes are followed?

259. Who is responsible for estimating the activity durations?

260. Are all attributes of the activities defined, including risk and uncertainty?

261. Are the appropriate IT resources adequate to meet planned commitments?

262. Have Enterprise Technology project team accountabilities & responsibilities been clearly defined?

263. Are vendor contract reports, reviews and visits

conducted periodically?

264. What does a valid Schedule look like?

265. Is an industry recognized mechanized support tool(s) being used for Enterprise Technology project scheduling & tracking?

266. Is the steering committee active in Enterprise Technology project oversight?

267. Are right task and resource calendars used in the IMS?

268. Are changes in deliverable commitments agreed to by all affected groups & individuals?

269. What is the estimated time to complete the Enterprise Technology project if status quo is maintained?

270. Is stakeholder involvement adequate?

271. Have all documents been archived in a Enterprise Technology project repository for each release?

272. Are procurement deliverables arriving on time and to specification?

2.11 Activity List: Enterprise Technology

273. How do you determine the late start (LS) for each activity?

274. What is the LF and LS for each activity?

275. Who will perform the work?

276. What is the probability the Enterprise Technology project can be completed in xx weeks?

277. What are you counting on?

278. What went right?

279. How should ongoing costs be monitored to try to keep the Enterprise Technology project within budget?

280. What did not go as well?

281. Are the required resources available or need to be acquired?

282. How can the Enterprise Technology project be displayed graphically to better visualize the activities?

283. Is infrastructure setup part of your Enterprise Technology project?

284. How much slack is available in the Enterprise

Technology project?

285. When do the individual activities need to start and finish?

286. What are the critical bottleneck activities?

287. How difficult will it be to do specific activities on this Enterprise Technology project?

288. Should you include sub-activities?

289. What went well?

290. For other activities, how much delay can be tolerated?

291. Where will it be performed?

2.12 Activity Attributes: Enterprise Technology

292. How many resources do you need to complete the work scope within a limit of X number of days?

293. Which method produces the more accurate cost assignment?

294. Has management defined a definite timeframe for the turnaround or Enterprise Technology project window?

295. How difficult will it be to do specific activities on this Enterprise Technology project?

296. Were there other ways you could have organized the data to achieve similar results?

297. Activity: what is Missing?

298. Activity: fair or not fair?

299. Have you identified the Activity Leveling Priority code value on each activity?

300. Are the required resources available?

301. Where else does it apply?

302. How do you manage time?

303. Can you re-assign any activities to another

resource to resolve an over-allocation?

304. How much activity detail is required?

305. Resource is assigned to?

306. Can more resources be added?

307. Do you feel very comfortable with your prediction?

308. Have constraints been applied to the start and finish milestones for the phases?

309. Activity: what is In the Bag?

310. Is there anything planned that does not need to be here?

2.13 Milestone List: Enterprise Technology

311. What background experience, skills, and strengths does the team bring to your organization?

312. Competitive advantages?

313. How soon can the activity start?

314. Which path is the critical path?

315. What is the market for your technology, product or service?

316. What is your organizations history in doing similar activities?

317. Insurmountable weaknesses?

318. How late can the activity finish?

319. Reliability of data, plan predictability?

320. What would happen if a delivery of material was one week late?

321. How will you get the word out to customers?

322. Sustainable financial backing?

323. Gaps in capabilities?

324. Describe the concept of the technology, product or service that will be or has been developed. How will it be used?

325. Level of the Innovation?

326. Vital contracts and partners?

327. What has been done so far?

328. How will the milestone be verified?

329. What are your competitors vulnerabilities?

2.14 Network Diagram: Enterprise Technology

330. What are the Key Success Factors?

331. What is the lowest cost to complete this Enterprise Technology project in xx weeks?

332. Exercise: what is the probability that the Enterprise Technology project duration will exceed xx weeks?

333. Where do schedules come from?

334. Review the logical flow of the network diagram. Take a look at which activities you have first and then sequence the activities. Do they make sense?

335. Where do you schedule uncertainty time?

336. What must be completed before an activity can be started?

337. What activities must occur simultaneously with this activity?

338. Planning: who, how long, what to do?

339. If x is long, what would be the completion time if you break x into two parallel parts of y weeks and z weeks?

340. What controls the start and finish of a job?

341. Why must you schedule milestones, such as reviews, throughout the Enterprise Technology project?

342. Are you on time?

343. What activity must be completed immediately before this activity can start?

344. If a current contract exists, can you provide the vendor name, contract start, and contract expiration date?

345. What activities must follow this activity?

346. What job or jobs could run concurrently?

347. What to do and When?

2.15 Activity Resource Requirements: Enterprise Technology

348. Time for overtime?

349. Are there unresolved issues that need to be addressed?

350. What are constraints that you might find during the Human Resource Planning process?

351. Do you use tools like decomposition and rolling-wave planning to produce the activity list and other outputs?

352. Other support in specific areas?

353. Why do you do that?

354. How do you handle petty cash?

355. When does monitoring begin?

356. How many signatures do you require on a check and does this match what is in your policy and procedures?

357. Organizational Applicability?

358. Anything else?

359. Which logical relationship does the PDM use most often?

360. What is the Work Plan Standard?

2.16 Resource Breakdown Structure: Enterprise Technology

361. Why time management?

362. Changes based on input from stakeholders?

363. Who will use the system?

364. What is each stakeholders desired outcome for the Enterprise Technology project?

365. How should the information be delivered?

366. Who is allowed to perform which functions?

367. How difficult will it be to do specific activities on this Enterprise Technology project?

368. Is predictive resource analysis being done?

369. How can this help you with team building?

370. Who is allowed to see what data about which resources?

371. Who needs what information?

372. What defines a successful Enterprise Technology project?

373. What went wrong?

374. What is the difference between % Complete and % work?

375. What is Enterprise Technology project communication management?

376. Which resources should be in the resource pool?

377. What is the number one predictor of a groups productivity?

2.17 Activity Duration Estimates: Enterprise Technology

378. What questions do you have about the sample documents provided?

379. What is the BEST thing for the Enterprise Technology project manager to do?

380. What is earned value?

381. What are the Enterprise Technology project management deliverables of each process group?

382. What Enterprise Technology project was the first to use modern Enterprise Technology project management?

383. Are updates on work results collected and used as inputs to the performance reporting process?

384. What are some general rules of thumb for deciding if cost variance, schedule variance, cost performance index, and schedule performance index numbers are good or bad?

385. What is the difference between conceptual, application, and evaluative questions?

386. How does Enterprise Technology project management relate to other disciplines?

387. What distinguishes one organization from

another in this area?

388. Write a oneto two-page paper describing your dream team for this Enterprise Technology project. What type of people would you want on your team?

389. Account for the four frames of organizations. How can they help Enterprise Technology project managers understand your organizational context for Enterprise Technology projects?

390. Are performance reviews conducted regularly to assess the status of Enterprise Technology projects?

391. What are some crucial elements of a good Enterprise Technology project plan?

392. What is involved in the solicitation process?

393. Are procurement documents used to solicit accurate and complete proposals from prospective sellers?

394. How do you enter durations, link tasks, and view critical path information?

395. If you plan to take the PMP exam soon, what should you do to prepare?

2.18 Duration Estimating Worksheet: Enterprise Technology

396. What utility impacts are there?

397. Is the Enterprise Technology project responsive to community need?

398. What is an Average Enterprise Technology project?

399. Does the Enterprise Technology project provide innovative ways for stakeholders to overcome obstacles or deliver better outcomes?

400. Value pocket identification & quantification what are value pockets?

401. What work will be included in the Enterprise Technology project?

402. Science = process: remember the scientific method?

403. Can the Enterprise Technology project be constructed as planned?

404. Is this operation cost effective?

405. What info is needed?

406. What is your role?

407. What is the total time required to complete the Enterprise Technology project if no delays occur?

408. Will the Enterprise Technology project collaborate with the local community and leverage resources?

409. How should ongoing costs be monitored to try to keep the Enterprise Technology project within budget?

410. Why estimate costs?

411. Small or large Enterprise Technology project?

2.19 Project Schedule: Enterprise Technology

412. Is the structure for tracking the Enterprise Technology project schedule well defined and assigned to a specific individual?

413. Is the Enterprise Technology project schedule available for all Enterprise Technology project team members to review?

414. Verify that the update is accurate. Are all remaining durations correct?

415. Are the original Enterprise Technology project schedule and budget realistic?

416. Are you working on the right risks?

417. Why do you need schedules?

418. Why is software Enterprise Technology project disaster so common?

419. Does the condition or event threaten the Enterprise Technology projects objectives in any ways?

420. Change management required?

421. What is the most mis-scheduled part of process?

422. How effectively were issues able to be resolved

without impacting the Enterprise Technology project Schedule or Budget?

423. Why do you need to manage Enterprise Technology project Risk?

424. Why or why not?

425. What is the purpose of a Enterprise Technology project schedule?

426. Your best shot for providing estimations how complex/how much work does the activity require?

427. To what degree is do you feel the entire team was committed to the Enterprise Technology project schedule?

428. Have all Enterprise Technology project delays been adequately accounted for, communicated to all stakeholders and adjustments made in overall Enterprise Technology project schedule?

429. Is there a Schedule Management Plan that establishes the criteria and activities for developing, monitoring and controlling the Enterprise Technology project schedule?

430. Are quality inspections and review activities listed in the Enterprise Technology project schedule(s)?

2.20 Cost Management Plan: Enterprise Technology

431. How does the proposed individual meet each requirement?

432. Are change requests logged and managed?

433. Quality assurance overheads?

434. Are risk triggers captured?

435. Is it a Enterprise Technology project?

436. Do Enterprise Technology project teams & team members report on status / activities / progress?

437. Have key stakeholders been identified?

438. What strengths do you have?

439. How do you manage cost?

440. What would you do differently what did not work?

441. Is the Enterprise Technology project schedule available for all Enterprise Technology project team members to review?

442. Are corrective actions and variances reported?

443. Are metrics used to evaluate and manage

Vendors?

444. Is there anything unique in this Enterprise Technology projects scope statement that will affect resources?

445. Are issues raised, assessed, actioned, and resolved in a timely and efficient manner?

446. Is there an on-going process in place to monitor Enterprise Technology project risks?

447. Contractors scope – how will contractors scope be defined when contracts are let?

448. Estimating responsibilities – how will the responsibilities for cost estimating be allocated?

449. Are vendor invoices audited for accuracy before payment?

2.21 Activity Cost Estimates: Enterprise Technology

450. Maintenance Reserve?

451. Were decisions made in a timely manner?

452. Where can you get activity reports?

453. Can you delete activities or make them inactive?

454. What skill level is required to do the job?

455. What is included in indirect cost being allocated?

456. What makes a good activity description?

457. What were things that you did very well and want to do the same again on the next Enterprise Technology project?

458. If you are asked to lower your estimate because the price is too high, what are your options?

459. What do you want to know about the stay to know if costs were inappropriately high or low?

460. In which phase of the acquisition process cycle does source qualifications reside?

461. What is your organizations history in doing similar tasks?

462. Are data needed on characteristics of care?

463. How do you treat administrative costs in the activity inventory?

464. How quickly can the task be done with the skills available?

465. How do you change activities?

466. Are cost subtotals needed?

467. One way to define activities is to consider how organization employees describe jobs to families and friends. You basically want to know, What do you do?

468. Does the activity rely on a common set of tools to carry it out?

2.22 Cost Estimating Worksheet: Enterprise Technology

469. What is the estimated labor cost today based upon this information?

470. Is the Enterprise Technology project responsive to community need?

471. Who is best positioned to know and assist in identifying corresponding factors?

472. Identify the timeframe necessary to monitor progress and collect data to determine how the selected measure has changed?

473. Ask: are others positioned to know, are others credible, and will others cooperate?

474. How will the results be shared and to whom?

475. What will others want?

476. What is the purpose of estimating?

477. What additional Enterprise Technology project(s) could be initiated as a result of this Enterprise Technology project?

478. What costs are to be estimated?

479. What happens to any remaining funds not used?

480. Will the Enterprise Technology project collaborate with the local community and leverage resources?

481. Can a trend be established from historical performance data on the selected measure and are the criteria for using trend analysis or forecasting methods met?

482. Does the Enterprise Technology project provide innovative ways for stakeholders to overcome obstacles or deliver better outcomes?

483. Is it feasible to establish a control group arrangement?

484. What can be included?

2.23 Cost Baseline: Enterprise Technology

485. What is it ?

486. What threats might prevent you from getting there?

487. On budget?

488. How likely is it to go wrong?

489. What can go wrong?

490. Have all approved changes to the Enterprise Technology project requirement been identified and impact on the performance, cost, and schedule baselines documented?

491. For what purpose ?

492. Is the requested change request a result of changes in other Enterprise Technology project(s)?

493. Has the Enterprise Technology project (or Enterprise Technology project phase) been evaluated against each objective established in the product description and Integrated Enterprise Technology project Plan?

494. When should cost estimates be developed?

495. How long are you willing to wait before you find

out were late?

496. Are there contingencies or conditions related to the acceptance?

497. Does a process exist for establishing a cost baseline to measure Enterprise Technology project performance?

498. What is the reality?

499. Vac -variance at completion, how much over/ under budget do you expect to be?

500. Is the cr within Enterprise Technology project scope?

501. Impact to environment?

502. What is the consequence?

503. What do you want to measure ?

2.24 Quality Management Plan: Enterprise Technology

504. What is the return on investment?

505. How are changes approved?

506. How is staff trained on the recording of field notes?

507. Are there processes in place to ensure internal consistency between the source code components?

508. Is the amount of effort justified by the anticipated value of forming a new process?

509. Can it be done better?

510. How does your organization determine the requirements and product/service features important to customers?

511. Who is approving the QAPP?

512. Do you periodically review your data quality system to see that it is up to date and appropriate?

513. How do your action plans support the strategic objectives?

514. What changes can you make that will result in improvement?

515. Does a documented Enterprise Technology project organizational policy & plan (i.e. governance model) exist?

516. How do you ensure that protocols are up to date?

517. Sampling part of task?

518. How does your organization use comparative data and information to improve organizational performance?

519. Who is responsible for writing the qapp?

520. Has a Enterprise Technology project Communications Plan been developed?

521. Are you meeting your customers expectations consistently?

2.25 Quality Metrics: Enterprise Technology

522. How do you know if everyone is trying to improve the right things?

523. When will the Final Guidance will be issued?

524. What group is empowered to define quality requirements?

525. How do you measure?

526. Is quality culture a competitive advantage?

527. What metrics do you measure?

528. What are you trying to accomplish?

529. Does risk analysis documentation meet standards?

530. Is there a set of procedures to capture, analyze and act on quality metrics?

531. Where is quality now?

532. What are your organizations expectations for its quality Enterprise Technology project?

533. Are quality metrics defined?

534. Are documents on hand to provide explanations

of privacy and confidentiality?

535. Is the reporting frequency appropriate?

536. What forces exist that would cause them to change?

537. What do you measure?

538. How are requirements conflicts resolved?

539. What level of statistical confidence do you use?

2.26 Process Improvement Plan: Enterprise Technology

540. Where are you now?

541. The motive is determined by asking, Why do you want to achieve this goal?

542. What is the test-cycle concept?

543. Why do you want to achieve the goal?

544. What personnel are the sponsors for that initiative?

545. Does explicit definition of the measures exist?

546. Everyone agrees on what process improvement is, right?

547. Has a process guide to collect the data been developed?

548. Where do you want to be?

549. Are there forms and procedures to collect and record the data?

550. What lessons have you learned so far?

551. Are you making progress on your improvement plan?

552. Why quality management?

553. What personnel are the coaches for your initiative?

554. Has the time line required to move measurement results from the points of collection to databases or users been established?

555. Are you meeting the quality standards?

556. Does your process ensure quality?

557. What personnel are the champions for the initiative?

558. If a process improvement framework is being used, which elements will help the problems and goals listed?

2.27 Responsibility Assignment Matrix: Enterprise Technology

559. What are the deliverables?

560. Are detailed work packages planned as far in advance as practicable?

561. Are control accounts opened and closed based on the start and completion of work contained therein?

562. Cwbs elements to be subcontracted, with identification of subcontractors?

563. Who is going to do that work?

564. What will the work cost?

565. When performing is split among two or more roles, is the work clearly defined so that the efforts are coordinated and the communication is clear?

566. Is data disseminated to the contractors management timely, accurate, and usable?

567. How do you manage remotely to staff in other Divisions?

568. Too many is: do all the identified roles need to be routinely informed or only in exceptional circumstances?

569. Does each activity-deliverable have exactly one Accountable responsibility, so that accountability is clear and decisions can be made quickly?

570. What is the purpose of assigning and documenting responsibility?

571. Is accountability placed at the lowest-possible level within the Enterprise Technology project so that decisions can be made at that level?

572. What tool can show you individual and group allocations?

573. Are too many reports done in writing instead of verbally?

574. Does a missing responsibility indicate that the current Enterprise Technology project is not yet fully understood?

2.28 Roles and Responsibilities: Enterprise Technology

575. Is the data complete?

576. What areas would you highlight for changes or improvements?

577. Was the expectation clearly communicated?

578. Who: who is involved?

579. Have you ever been a part of this team?

580. Authority: what areas/Enterprise Technology projects in your work do you have the authority to decide upon and act on the already stated decisions?

581. What should you do now to prepare for your career 5+ years from now?

582. What should you do now to ensure that you are exceeding expectations and excelling in your current position?

583. Is feedback clearly communicated and non-judgmental?

584. Do the values and practices inherent in the culture of your organization foster or hinder the process?

585. What expectations were NOT met?

586. What should you highlight for improvement?

587. Once the responsibilities are defined for the Enterprise Technology project, have the deliverables, roles and responsibilities been clearly communicated to every participant?

588. Attainable / achievable: the goal is attainable; can you actually accomplish the goal?

589. Do you take the time to clearly define roles and responsibilities on Enterprise Technology project tasks?

590. What expectations were met?

591. Are governance roles and responsibilities documented?

592. Who is responsible for implementation activities and where will the functions, roles and responsibilities be defined?

2.29 Human Resource Management Plan: Enterprise Technology

593. Is quality monitored from the perspective of the customers needs and expectations?

594. Are trade-offs between accepting the risk and mitigating the risk identified?

595. Is there a formal set of procedures supporting Issues Management?

596. Is a payment system in place with proper reviews and approvals?

597. What were things that you did very well and want to do the same again on the next Enterprise Technology project?

598. Is the assigned Enterprise Technology project manager a PMP (Certified Enterprise Technology project manager) and experienced?

599. Is the Enterprise Technology project schedule available for all Enterprise Technology project team members to review?

600. What is this Enterprise Technology project aiming to achieve?

601. Were the budget estimates reasonable?

602. Are people motivated to meet the current and

future challenges?

603. Are adequate resources provided for the quality assurance function?

604. Has a resource management plan been created?

605. Are estimating assumptions and constraints captured?

606. Were escalated issues resolved promptly?

607. Timeline and milestones?

608. Is it standard practice to formally commit stakeholders to the Enterprise Technology project via agreements?

609. Is an industry recognized support tool(s) being used for Enterprise Technology project scheduling & tracking?

610. Are internal Enterprise Technology project status meetings held at reasonable intervals?

611. Has the schedule been baselined?

2.30 Communications Management Plan: Enterprise Technology

612. Are stakeholders internal or external?

613. What are the interrelationships?

614. Are there common objectives between the team and the stakeholder?

615. What data is going to be required?

616. Is there an important stakeholder who is actively opposed and will not receive messages?

617. What help do you and your team need from the stakeholder?

618. Are others part of the communications management plan?

619. How did the term stakeholder originate?

620. Why manage stakeholders?

621. Who to share with?

622. Can you think of other people who might have concerns or interests?

623. Conflict resolution -which method when?

624. How much time does it take to do it?

625. What is the stakeholders level of authority?

626. Do you feel a register helps?

627. What to learn?

628. Do you then often overlook a key stakeholder or stakeholder group?

629. Who will use or be affected by the result of a Enterprise Technology project?

630. How often do you engage with stakeholders?

631. What approaches to you feel are the best ones to use?

2.31 Risk Management Plan: Enterprise Technology

632. Are the participants able to keep up with the workload?

633. What will drive change?

634. Monitoring -what factors can you track that will enable you to determine if the risk is becoming more or less likely?

635. What did not work so well?

636. Is the process being followed?

637. Are testing tools available and suitable?

638. Risks should be identified during which phase of Enterprise Technology project management life cycle?

639. My Enterprise Technology project leader has suddenly left your organization, what do you do?

640. Is there additional information that would make you more confident about your analysis?

641. What are the cost, schedule and resource impacts of avoiding the risk?

642. Can you stabilize dynamic risk factors?

643. Financial risk -can your organization afford to

undertake the Enterprise Technology project?

644. Does the customer understand the software process?

645. What things are likely to change?

646. How is the audit profession changing?

647. Are the best people available?

648. Is this an issue, action item, question or a risk?

649. Is the customer technically sophisticated in the product area?

650. Are flexibility and reuse paramount?

651. What are some questions that should be addressed in a risk management plan?

2.32 Risk Register: Enterprise Technology

652. Do you require further engagement?

653. Are your objectives at risk?

654. Schedule impact/severity estimated range (workdays) assume the event happens, what is the potential impact?

655. What could prevent you delivering on the strategic program objectives and what is being done to mitigate corresponding issues?

656. What further options might be available for responding to the risk?

657. What are the assumptions and current status that support the assessment of the risk?

658. How is a Community Risk Register created?

659. Are there any gaps in the evidence?

660. Who is going to do it?

661. Risk documentation: what reporting formats and processes will be used for risk management activities?

662. Cost/benefit – how much will the proposed mitigations cost and how does this cost compare with the potential cost of the risk event/situation should it

occur?

663. What is a Community Risk Register?

664. Market risk -will the new service or product be useful to your organization or marketable to others?

665. Technology risk -is the Enterprise Technology project technically feasible?

666. What are the major risks facing the Enterprise Technology project?

667. What is the appropriate level of risk management for this Enterprise Technology project?

668. Contingency actions - planned actions to reduce the immediate seriousness of the risk when it does occur. What should you do when?

669. Budget and schedule: what are the estimated costs and schedules for performing risk-related activities?

670. What risks might negatively or positively affect achieving the Enterprise Technology project objectives?

2.33 Probability and Impact Assessment: Enterprise Technology

671. What is the risk appetite?

672. Are tools for analysis and design available?

673. Does the Enterprise Technology project team have experience with the technology to be implemented?

674. Monitoring of the overall Enterprise Technology project status – are there any changes in the Enterprise Technology project that can effect and cause new possible risks?

675. Sensitivity analysis -which risks will have the most impact on the Enterprise Technology project?

676. How do risks change during the Enterprise Technology projects life cycle?

677. What is the likelihood?

678. Does the customer have a solid idea of what is required?

679. Do you have specific methods that you use for each phase of the process?

680. My Enterprise Technology project leader has suddenly left your organization, what do you do?

681. What will be the environmental impact of the Enterprise Technology project?

682. Is the customer willing to establish rapid communication links with the developer?

683. Is a software Enterprise Technology project management tool available?

684. What are the preparations required for facing difficulties?

685. Are end-users enthusiastically committed to the Enterprise Technology project and the system/ product to be built?

686. Anticipated volatility of the requirements?

687. What kind of preparation would be required to do this?

688. Do you use diagramming techniques to show cause and effect?

2.34 Probability and Impact Matrix: Enterprise Technology

689. What action do you usually take against risks?

690. Will there be an increase in the political conservatism?

691. How can you understand and diagnose risks and identify sources?

692. How do you define a risk?

693. What is the likely future demand of the customer?

694. If you can not fix it, how do you do it differently?

695. Is the Enterprise Technology project cutting across the entire organization?

696. Is the number of people on the Enterprise Technology project team adequate to do the job?

697. How to prioritize risks?

698. Have customers been involved fully in the definition of requirements?

699. Mandated delivery date?

700. Are the risk data timely and relevant?

701. What is the industrial relations prevailing in this organization?

702. Degree of confidence in estimated size estimate?

703. What risks are necessary to achieve success?

704. Do requirements put excessive performance constraints on the product?

705. Risk may be made during which step of risk management?

2.35 Risk Data Sheet: Enterprise Technology

706. What were the Causes that contributed?

707. Type of risk identified?

708. What are you weak at and therefore need to do better?

709. What if client refuses?

710. How can it happen?

711. What is the likelihood of it happening?

712. What is the chance that it will happen?

713. What do you know?

714. Will revised controls lead to tolerable risk levels?

715. Has a sensitivity analysis been carried out?

716. How can hazards be reduced?

717. Potential for recurrence?

718. What are the main threats to your existence?

719. What is the environment within which you operate (social trends, economic, community values, broad based participation, national directions etc.)?

720. Who has a vested interest in how you perform as your organization (our stakeholders)?

721. What was measured?

722. Risk of what?

723. Is the data sufficiently specified in terms of the type of failure being analyzed, and its frequency or probability?

2.36 Procurement Management Plan: Enterprise Technology

724. Was an original risk assessment/risk management plan completed?

725. Does the resource management plan include a personnel development plan?

726. Are quality inspections and review activities listed in the Enterprise Technology project schedule(s)?

727. Are assumptions being identified, recorded, analyzed, qualified and closed?

728. Do Enterprise Technology project managers participating in the Enterprise Technology project know the Enterprise Technology projects true status first hand?

729. Has your organization readiness assessment been conducted?

730. Is there any form of automated support for Issues Management?

731. Was your organizations estimating methodology being used and followed?

732. Are the payment terms being followed?

733. Are actuals compared against estimates to

analyze and correct variances?

734. Are meeting objectives identified for each meeting?

735. Are meeting minutes captured and sent out after meetings?

736. Are internal Enterprise Technology project status meetings held at reasonable intervals?

737. Have Enterprise Technology project management standards and procedures been identified / established and documented?

738. What were things that you did well, and could improve, and how?

739. Is Enterprise Technology project status reviewed with the steering and executive teams at appropriate intervals?

740. Is it standard practice to formally commit stakeholders to the Enterprise Technology project via agreements?

741. Does the Enterprise Technology project have a formal Enterprise Technology project Charter?

742. Is a pmo (Enterprise Technology project management office) in place which provides oversight to the Enterprise Technology project?

2.37 Source Selection Criteria: Enterprise Technology

743. What are the special considerations for preaward debriefings?

744. Are considerations anticipated?

745. Is a letter of commitment from each proposed team member and key subcontractor included?

746. Does an evaluation need to include the identification of strengths and weaknesses?

747. When is it appropriate to issue a DRFP?

748. What benefits are accrued from issuing a DRFP in advance of issuing a final RFP?

749. Who should attend debriefings?

750. How can the methods of publicizing the buy be tailored to yield more effective price competition?

751. Why promote competition?

752. Can you identify proposed teaming partners and/or subcontractors and consider the nature and extent of proposed involvement in satisfying the Enterprise Technology project requirements?

753. Do proposed hours support content and schedule?

754. What should be the contracting officers strategy?

755. How can solicitation Schedules be improved to yield more effective price competition?

756. What does a sample rating scale look like?

757. Do you consider all weaknesses, significant weaknesses, and deficiencies?

758. How do you consolidate reviews and analysis of evaluators?

759. How should the solicitation aspects regarding past performance be structured?

760. How will you decide an evaluators write up is sufficient?

761. What are open book debriefings?

2.38 Stakeholder Management Plan: Enterprise Technology

762. Will the current technology alter during the life of the Enterprise Technology project?

763. Contradictory information between document sections?

764. Is the quality assurance team identified?

765. Which of the records created within the Enterprise Technology project, if any, does the Business Owner require access to?

766. Is an industry recognized mechanized support tool(s) being used for Enterprise Technology project scheduling & tracking?

767. Is the communication plan being followed?

768. Has the Enterprise Technology project manager been identified?

769. How are you doing/what can be done better?

770. Have the procedures for identifying budget variances been followed?

771. Are Enterprise Technology project contact logs kept up to date?

772. Do Enterprise Technology project teams & team

members report on status / activities / progress?

773. Has the scope management document been updated and distributed to help prevent scope creep?

774. Are there any potential occupational health and safety issues due to the proposed purchases?

775. Are Enterprise Technology project contact logs kept up to date?

776. Who is responsible for the post implementation review process?

777. Are formal code reviews conducted?

2.39 Change Management Plan: Enterprise Technology

778. When does it make sense to customize?

779. Will the readiness criteria be met prior to the training roll out?

780. Who will fund the training?

781. Would you need to tailor a special message for each segment of the audience?

782. What time commitment will this involve?

783. Has a training need analysis been carried out?

784. How will the stakeholders share information and transfer knowledge?

785. Has the priority for this Enterprise Technology project been set by the Business Unit Management Team?

786. Who might be able to help you the most?

787. Who will be the change levers?

788. Who might present the most resistance?

789. What processes are in place to manage knowledge about the Enterprise Technology project?

790. Why is the initiative is being undertaken - What are the business drivers?

791. Have the systems been configured and tested?

792. Will a different work structure focus people on what is important?

793. How prevalent is Resistance to Change?

794. Which relationships will change?

3.0 Executing Process Group: Enterprise Technology

795. Does the Enterprise Technology project team have the right skills?

796. Could a new application negatively affect the current IT infrastructure?

797. What are the main types of goods and services being outsourced?

798. Is the Enterprise Technology project making progress in helping to achieve the set results?

799. It under budget or over budget?

800. What are the main types of contracts if you do decide to outsource?

801. How will professionals learn what is expected from them what the deliverables are?

802. Is the program supported by national and/or local organizations?

803. Were sponsors and decision makers available when needed outside regularly scheduled meetings?

804. How will you avoid scope creep?

805. On which process should team members spend the most time?

806. How is Enterprise Technology project performance information created and distributed?

807. What areas does the group agree are the biggest success on the Enterprise Technology project?

808. How well did the team follow the chosen processes?

809. What are deliverables of your Enterprise Technology project?

810. Based on your Enterprise Technology project communication management plan, what worked well?

811. Will outside resources be needed to help?

812. Does the Enterprise Technology project team have enough people to execute the Enterprise Technology project plan?

813. What is the shortest possible time it will take to complete this Enterprise Technology project?

3.1 Team Member Status Report: Enterprise Technology

814. When a teams productivity and success depend on collaboration and the efficient flow of information, what generally fails them?

815. Is there evidence that staff is taking a more professional approach toward management of your organizations Enterprise Technology projects?

816. What specific interest groups do you have in place?

817. How will resource planning be done?

818. Do you have an Enterprise Enterprise Technology project Management Office (EPMO)?

819. The problem with Reward & Recognition Programs is that the truly deserving people all too often get left out. How can you make it practical?

820. Are the products of your organizations Enterprise Technology projects meeting customers objectives?

821. How can you make it practical?

822. Does every department have to have a Enterprise Technology project Manager on staff?

823. Are the attitudes of staff regarding Enterprise Technology project work improving?

824. How much risk is involved?

825. How does this product, good, or service meet the needs of the Enterprise Technology project and your organization as a whole?

826. Are your organizations Enterprise Technology projects more successful over time?

827. Why is it to be done?

828. How it is to be done?

829. What is to be done?

830. Will the staff do training or is that done by a third party?

831. Does the product, good, or service already exist within your organization?

832. Does your organization have the means (staff, money, contract, etc.) to produce or to acquire the product, good, or service?

3.2 Change Request: Enterprise Technology

833. Who is included in the change control team?

834. Why were your requested changes rejected or not made?

835. Are there requirements attributes that are strongly related to the complexity and size?

836. What should be regulated in a change control operating instruction?

837. How shall the implementation of changes be recorded?

838. Will all change requests and current status be logged?

839. What has an inspector to inspect and to check?

840. When to submit a change request?

841. How are changes requested (forms, method of communication)?

842. Who is communicating the change?

843. Who can suggest changes?

844. Can static requirements change attributes like the size of the change be used to predict reliability in

execution?

845. Should a more thorough impact analysis be conducted?

846. How does a team identify the discrete elements of a configuration?

847. Who is responsible to authorize changes?

848. Who is responsible for the implementation and monitoring of all measures?

849. What can be filed?

850. Will this change conflict with other requirements changes (e.g., lead to conflicting operational scenarios)?

851. How do you get changes (code) out in a timely manner?

3.3 Change Log: Enterprise Technology

852. How does this change affect scope?

853. How does this relate to the standards developed for specific business processes?

854. When was the request approved?

855. Where do changes come from?

856. How does this change affect the timeline of the schedule?

857. Is the submitted change a new change or a modification of a previously approved change?

858. Do the described changes impact on the integrity or security of the system?

859. Does the suggested change request represent a desired enhancement to the products functionality?

860. Is the requested change request a result of changes in other Enterprise Technology project(s)?

861. Is the change request open, closed or pending?

862. Who initiated the change request?

863. Is the change backward compatible without limitations?

864. Will the Enterprise Technology project fail if the change request is not executed?

865. Is the change request within Enterprise Technology project scope?

866. When was the request submitted?

867. Does the suggested change request seem to represent a necessary enhancement to the product?

868. Is this a mandatory replacement?

3.4 Decision Log: Enterprise Technology

869. Linked to original objective?

870. It becomes critical to track and periodically revisit both operational effectiveness; Are you noticing all that you need to, and are you interpreting what you see effectively?

871. Is your opponent open to a non-traditional workflow, or will it likely challenge anything you do?

872. Do strategies and tactics aimed at less than full control reduce the costs of management or simply shift the cost burden?

873. What makes you different or better than others companies selling the same thing?

874. What is the average size of your matters in an applicable measurement?

875. Adversarial environment. is your opponent open to a non-traditional workflow, or will it likely challenge anything you do?

876. Behaviors; what are guidelines that the team has identified that will assist them with getting the most out of team meetings?

877. Who is the decisionmaker?

878. What eDiscovery problem or issue did your organization set out to fix or make better?

879. With whom was the decision shared or considered?

880. Which variables make a critical difference?

881. Meeting purpose; why does this team meet?

882. What is your overall strategy for quality control / quality assurance procedures?

883. What alternatives/risks were considered?

884. How does an increasing emphasis on cost containment influence the strategies and tactics used?

885. Who will be given a copy of this document and where will it be kept?

886. At what point in time does loss become unacceptable?

887. How effective is maintaining the log at facilitating organizational learning?

888. What was the rationale for the decision?

3.5 Quality Audit: Enterprise Technology

889. How does your organization know that its support services planning and management systems are appropriately effective and constructive?

890. Are the review comments incorporated?

891. How does your organization know that its staff embody the core knowledge, skills and characteristics for which it wishes to be recognized?

892. How does your organization know that its management of its ethical responsibilities is appropriately effective and constructive?

893. Are people allowed to contribute ideas?

894. What will the Observer get to Observe?

895. What does an analysis of your organizations staff profile suggest in terms of its planning, and how is this being addressed?

896. Do prior clients have a positive opinion of your organization?

897. Does the supplier use a formal quality system?

898. How does your organization know that its Mission, Vision and Values Statements are appropriate and effectively guiding your organization?

899. How does your organization know that it is effectively and constructively guiding staff through to timely completion of tasks?

900. How does your organization know that the support for its staff is appropriately effective and constructive?

901. How does your organization know whether they are adhering to mission and achieving objectives?

902. Are salvageable and salvaged medical devices stored in a manner to prevent damage and/or contamination?

903. What data about organizational performance is routinely collected and reported?

904. How does your organization know that its management system is appropriately effective and constructive?

905. Have the risks associated with the intentions been identified, analyzed and appropriate responses developed?

906. Are all records associated with the reconditioning of a device maintained for a minimum of two years after the sale or disposal of the last device within a lot of merchandise?

907. How does your organization know that it provides a safe and healthy environment?

908. What experience do staff have in the type of work

that the audit entails?

3.6 Team Directory: Enterprise Technology

909. Who will report Enterprise Technology project status to all stakeholders?

910. Does a Enterprise Technology project team directory list all resources assigned to the Enterprise Technology project?

911. Process decisions: which organizational elements and which individuals will be assigned management functions?

912. Process decisions: do job conditions warrant additional actions to collect job information and document on-site activity?

913. Where should the information be distributed?

914. Who are the Team Members?

915. How and in what format should information be presented?

916. What are you going to deliver or accomplish?

917. When will you produce deliverables?

918. Process decisions: how well was task order work performed?

919. How do unidentified risks impact the outcome of

the Enterprise Technology project?

920. Who will be the stakeholders on your next Enterprise Technology project?

921. Process decisions: are there any statutory or regulatory issues relevant to the timely execution of work?

922. Process decisions: is work progressing on schedule and per contract requirements?

923. Have you decided when to celebrate the Enterprise Technology projects completion date?

924. Do purchase specifications and configurations match requirements?

925. Process decisions: are all start-up, turn over and close out requirements of the contract satisfied?

926. Who is the Sponsor?

927. Who should receive information (all stakeholders)?

3.7 Team Operating Agreement: Enterprise Technology

928. What is a Virtual Team?

929. Do you send out the agenda and meeting materials in advance?

930. What is group supervision?

931. How do you want to be thought of and known within your organization?

932. What are the current caseload numbers in the unit?

933. What are the safety issues/risks that need to be addressed and/or that the team needs to consider?

934. Resource allocation: how will individual team members account for time and expenses, and how will this be allocated in the team budget?

935. What is the number of cases currently teamed?

936. Do you leverage technology engagement tools group chat, polls, screen sharing, etc.?

937. Do you begin with a question to engage everyone?

938. Do team members reside in more than two countries?

939. How will group handle unplanned absences?

940. Methodologies: how will key team processes be implemented, such as training, research, work deliverable production, review and approval processes, knowledge management, and meeting procedures?

941. Has the appropriate access to relevant data and analysis capability been granted?

942. How does teaming fit in with overall organizational goals and meet organizational needs?

943. The method to be used in the decision making process; Will it be consensus, majority rule, or the supervisor having the final say?

944. Do you listen for voice tone and word choice to understand the meaning behind words?

945. Do you prevent individuals from dominating the meeting?

946. Does your team need access to all documents and information at all times?

947. What is culture?

3.8 Team Performance Assessment: Enterprise Technology

948. To what degree can the team ensure that all members are individually and jointly accountable for the teams purpose, goals, approach, and work-products?

949. To what degree is there a sense that only the team can succeed?

950. To what degree will team members, individually and collectively, commit time to help themselves and others learn and develop skills?

951. Where to from here?

952. To what degree can team members vigorously define the teams purpose in considerations with others who are not part of the functioning team?

953. Individual task proficiency and team process behavior: what is important for team functioning?

954. What makes opportunities more or less obvious?

955. How hard did you try to make a good selection?

956. Do you promptly inform members about major developments that may affect them?

957. Does more radicalness mean more perceived benefits?

958. What are teams?

959. When does the medium matter?

960. Lack of method variance in self-reported affect and perceptions at work: Reality or artifact?

961. To what degree does the teams work approach provide opportunity for members to engage in results-based evaluation?

962. To what degree do the goals specify concrete team work products?

963. To what degree can team members meet frequently enough to accomplish the teams ends?

964. To what degree are fresh input and perspectives systematically caught and added (for example, through information and analysis, new members, and senior sponsors)?

965. Do you give group members authority to make at least some important decisions?

966. How do you manage human resources?

967. If you have criticized someones work for method variance in your role as reviewer, what was the circumstance?

3.9 Team Member Performance Assessment: Enterprise Technology

968. To what degree do team members understand one anothers roles and skills?

969. What qualities does a successful Team leader possess?

970. What is the role of the Reviewer?

971. What variables that affect team members achievement are within your control?

972. How was the determination made for which training platforms would be used (i.e., media selection)?

973. What evidence supports your decision-making?

974. Is it clear how goals will be accomplished?

975. How are performance measures and associated incentives developed?

976. To what degree do members articulate the goals beyond the team membership?

977. What is collaboration?

978. Who they are?

979. To what degree will new and supplemental skills

be introduced as the need is recognized?

980. To what extent did the evaluation influence the instructional path, such as with adaptive testing?

981. To what degree are the skill areas critical to team performance present?

982. To what extent are systems and applications (e.g., game engine, mobile device platform) utilized?

983. How do you create a self-sustaining capacity for a collaborative culture?

984. What changes do you need to make to align practices with beliefs?

985. To what degree are the teams goals and objectives clear, simple, and measurable?

986. To what degree can team members frequently and easily communicate with one another?

987. What innovations (if any) are developed to realize goals?

3.10 Issue Log: Enterprise Technology

988. What steps can you take for positive relationships?

989. What is the stakeholders political influence?

990. Are the Enterprise Technology project issues uniquely identified, including to which product they refer?

991. Why do you manage communications?

992. Who needs to know and how much?

993. Who is involved as you identify stakeholders?

994. Who have you worked with in past, similar initiatives?

995. What are the typical contents?

996. What is the status of the issue?

997. What effort will a change need?

998. What is the impact on the risks?

999. Who reported the issue?

1000. What is a Stakeholder?

1001. Who do you turn to if you have questions?

1002. Are they needed?

1003. What date was the issue resolved?

4.0 Monitoring and Controlling Process Group: Enterprise Technology

1004. Is there adequate validation on required fields?

1005. How to ensure validity, quality and consistency?

1006. Who needs to be engaged upfront to ensure use of results?

1007. Do clients benefit (change) from the services?

1008. How is agile portfolio management done?

1009. Feasibility: how much money, time, and effort can you put into this?

1010. Mitigate. what will you do to minimize the impact should a risk event occur?

1011. How can you monitor progress?

1012. Are the services being delivered?

1013. When will the Enterprise Technology project be done?

1014. Specific - is the objective clear in terms of what, how, when, and where the situation will be changed?

1015. Do the products created live up to the necessary quality?

1016. How well did the chosen processes fit the needs of the Enterprise Technology project?

1017. Did the Enterprise Technology project team have enough people to execute the Enterprise Technology project plan?

1018. What resources are necessary?

1019. Who are the Enterprise Technology project stakeholders?

1020. What factors are contributing to progress or delay in the achievement of products and results?

1021. What were things that you did very well and want to do the same again on the next Enterprise Technology project?

1022. What communication items need improvement?

1023. How many more potential communications channels were introduced by the discovery of the new stakeholders?

4.1 Project Performance Report: Enterprise Technology

1024. What is the degree to which rules govern information exchange between individuals within your organization?

1025. To what degree does the funding match the requirement?

1026. To what degree do all members feel responsible for all agreed-upon measures?

1027. To what degree will the team ensure that all members equitably share the work essential to the success of the team?

1028. To what degree are the structures of the formal organization consistent with the behaviors in the informal organization?

1029. To what degree do the relationships of the informal organization motivate taskrelevant behavior and facilitate task completion?

1030. To what degree do team members articulate the teams work approach?

1031. To what degree can all members engage in open and interactive considerations?

1032. To what degree does the teams approach to its work allow for modification and improvement over time?

1033. To what degree does the informal organization make use of individual resources and meet individual needs?

1034. To what degree does the information network provide individuals with the information they require?

1035. To what degree is the team cognizant of small wins to be celebrated along the way?

1036. To what degree is there centralized control of information sharing?

1037. To what degree are the goals realistic?

1038. To what degree does the information network communicate information relevant to the task?

1039. To what degree are the demands of the task compatible with and converge with the mission and functions of the formal organization?

4.2 Variance Analysis: Enterprise Technology

1040. What is the actual cost of work performed?

1041. What can be the cause of an increase in costs?

1042. Who are responsible for overhead performance control of related costs?

1043. Other relevant issues of Variance Analysis -selling price or gross margin?

1044. Who are responsible for the establishment of budgets and assignment of resources for overhead performance?

1045. Wbs elements contractually specified for reporting of status to your organization (lowest level only)?

1046. Are material costs reported within the same period as that in which BCWP is earned for that material?

1047. What are the actual costs to date?

1048. Is work properly classified as measured effort, LOE, or apportioned effort and appropriately separated?

1049. Contemplated overhead expenditure for each period based on the best information currently is available?

1050. Does the contractors system provide unit or lot costs when applicable?

1051. How are variances affected by multiple material and labor categories?

1052. Who is generally responsible for monitoring and taking action on variances?

1053. Are there quarterly budgets with quarterly performance comparisons?

1054. What costs are avoidable if one or more customers are dropped?

1055. Are significant decision points, constraints, and interfaces identified as key milestones?

4.3 Earned Value Status: Enterprise Technology

1056. Where are your problem areas?

1057. Earned value can be used in almost any Enterprise Technology project situation and in almost any Enterprise Technology project environment. it may be used on large Enterprise Technology projects, medium sized Enterprise Technology projects, tiny Enterprise Technology projects (in cut-down form), complex and simple Enterprise Technology projects and in any market sector. some people, of course, know all about earned value, they have used it for years - but perhaps not as effectively as they could have?

1058. When is it going to finish?

1059. If earned value management (EVM) is so good in determining the true status of a Enterprise Technology project and Enterprise Technology project its completion, why is it that hardly any one uses it in information systems related Enterprise Technology projects?

1060. What is the unit of forecast value?

1061. Where is evidence-based earned value in your organization reported?

1062. Verification is a process of ensuring that the developed system satisfies the stakeholders agreements and specifications; Are you building the product right? What do you verify?

1063. How much is it going to cost by the finish?

1064. Are you hitting your Enterprise Technology projects targets?

1065. Validation is a process of ensuring that the developed system will actually achieve the stakeholders desired outcomes; Are you building the right product? What do you validate?

1066. How does this compare with other Enterprise Technology projects?

4.4 Risk Audit: Enterprise Technology

1067. What are the outcomes you are looking for?

1068. Is a software Enterprise Technology project management tool available?

1069. Are you aware of the industry standards that apply to your operations?

1070. How do you compare to other jurisdictions when managing the risk of ....?

1071. What are the risks that could stop you from achieving your objectives?

1072. Do staff understand the extent of duty of care?

1073. Are corresponding safety and risk management policies posted for all to see?

1074. What is the implication of budget constraint on this process?

1075. What are the strategic implications with clients when auditors focus audit resources based on business-level risks?

1076. Is your organization able to present documentary evidence in support of compliance?

1077. For paid staff, does your organization comply with the minimum conditions for employment and/or the applicable modern award?

1078. Are all managers or operators of the facility or equipment competent or qualified?

1079. What is the Board doing to assure measurement and improve outcomes and quality and reduce avoidable adverse events?

1080. What are the Internal Controls ?

1081. What does monitoring consist of?

1082. Do all coaches/instructors/leaders have appropriate and current accreditation?

1083. The halo effect in business risk audits: can strategic risk assessment bias auditor judgment about accounting details?

1084. Have staff received necessary training?

1085. To what extent should analytical procedures be utilized in the risk-assessment process?

4.5 Contractor Status Report: Enterprise Technology

1086. What was the budget or estimated cost for your organizations services?

1087. What was the overall budget or estimated cost?

1088. What are the minimum and optimal bandwidth requirements for the proposed solution?

1089. Who can list a Enterprise Technology project as organization experience, your organization or a previous employee of your organization?

1090. If applicable; describe your standard schedule for new software version releases. Are new software version releases included in the standard maintenance plan?

1091. Describe how often regular updates are made to the proposed solution. Are corresponding regular updates included in the standard maintenance plan?

1092. What was the actual budget or estimated cost for your organizations services?

1093. What process manages the contracts?

1094. How is risk transferred?

1095. Are there contractual transfer concerns?

1096. How long have you been using the services?

1097. What was the final actual cost?

1098. What is the average response time for answering a support call?

4.6 Formal Acceptance: Enterprise Technology

1099. What was done right?

1100. What features, practices, and processes proved to be strengths or weaknesses?

1101. Does it do what Enterprise Technology project team said it would?

1102. Have all comments been addressed?

1103. Was the Enterprise Technology project managed well?

1104. Was business value realized?

1105. Do you perform formal acceptance or burn-in tests?

1106. Is formal acceptance of the Enterprise Technology project product documented and distributed?

1107. Was the sponsor/customer satisfied?

1108. Does it do what client said it would?

1109. Was the Enterprise Technology project goal achieved?

1110. What can you do better next time?

1111. Was the client satisfied with the Enterprise Technology project results?

1112. What are the requirements against which to test, Who will execute?

1113. General estimate of the costs and times to complete the Enterprise Technology project?

1114. Do you buy pre-configured systems or build your own configuration?

1115. Did the Enterprise Technology project achieve its MOV?

1116. What lessons were learned about your Enterprise Technology project management methodology?

1117. How well did the team follow the methodology?

1118. What is the Acceptance Management Process?

5.0 Closing Process Group: Enterprise Technology

1119. How will staff learn how to use the deliverables?

1120. How will you do it?

1121. Were cost budgets met?

1122. Are there funding or time constraints?

1123. Will the Enterprise Technology project deliverable(s) replace a current asset or group of assets?

1124. Is there a clear cause and effect between the activity and the lesson learned?

1125. Was the schedule met?

1126. Did you do things well?

1127. Does the close educate others to improve performance?

1128. Is this a follow-on to a previous Enterprise Technology project?

1129. What is the risk of failure to your organization?

1130. How well did the chosen processes fit the needs of the Enterprise Technology project?

1131. What is the amount of funding and what Enterprise Technology project phases are funded?

1132. What could have been improved?

1133. What could be done to improve the process?

1134. How critical is the Enterprise Technology project success to the success of your organization?

5.1 Procurement Audit: Enterprise Technology

1135. Is your organization aware and informed about international procurement standards and good practice?

1136. Is it on a regular basis examined whether it is possible to enter into public private partnerships with private suppliers?

1137. Can changes be made to automatic disbursement programs without proper approval of management?

1138. Was the performance description adequate to needs and legal requirements?

1139. Are the number of checking accounts where cash segregation is not required kept to a reasonable number?

1140. How do you assess whether the technical and financial evaluation was done properly and in fair manner?

1141. Has an upper limit of cost been fixed?

1142. Did the contracting authority offer unrestricted and full electronic access to the contract documents and any supplementary documents (specifying the internet address in the notice)?

1143. Were results of the award procedures published?

1144. Are petty cash funds operated on an imprest basis?

1145. Which are the main risks and controls of each phase?

1146. Did the chosen procedure ensure fair competition and transparency?

1147. Is there a policy on making purchases locally where possible?

1148. Are internal control systems in place?

1149. Are staff members evaluated in accordance with the terms of existing negotiated agreements?

1150. Is each copy of the purchase order necessary?

1151. Was the admissibility of variants displayed in the contract notice?

1152. Where an electronic auction was used to bid, were all required specifications given equally to tenderers?

1153. Are buyers prohibited from accepting gifts from vendors?

1154. Are receiving reports on file for all claims for equipment, supplies and materials in the paid claims file?

5.2 Contract Close-Out: Enterprise Technology

1155. Parties: Authorized?

1156. Are the signers the authorized officials?

1157. Have all acceptance criteria been met prior to final payment to contractors?

1158. How does it work?

1159. What is capture management?

1160. How is the contracting office notified of the automatic contract close-out?

1161. Have all contracts been completed?

1162. Change in circumstances?

1163. Have all contract records been included in the Enterprise Technology project archives?

1164. Has each contract been audited to verify acceptance and delivery?

1165. Parties: who is involved?

1166. How/when used ?

1167. Was the contract type appropriate?

1168. What happens to the recipient of services?

1169. Change in knowledge?

1170. Have all contracts been closed?

1171. Change in attitude or behavior?

1172. Was the contract sufficiently clear so as not to result in numerous disputes and misunderstandings?

1173. Was the contract complete without requiring numerous changes and revisions?

5.3 Project or Phase Close-Out: Enterprise Technology

1174. What is a Risk?

1175. What was expected from each stakeholder?

1176. Who controlled the resources for the Enterprise Technology project?

1177. What advantages do the an individual interview have over a group meeting, and vice-versa?

1178. Were the outcomes different from the already stated planned?

1179. Were risks identified and mitigated?

1180. What was learned?

1181. What are the marketing communication needs for each stakeholder?

1182. What information did each stakeholder need to contribute to the Enterprise Technology projects success?

1183. What is the information level of detail required for each stakeholder?

1184. What process was planned for managing issues/ risks?

1185. Planned remaining costs?

1186. Which changes might a stakeholder be required to make as a result of the Enterprise Technology project?

1187. Can the lesson learned be replicated?

1188. Planned completion date?

1189. When and how were information needs best met?

1190. Who exerted influence that has positively affected or negatively impacted the Enterprise Technology project?

1191. What benefits or impacts does the stakeholder group expect to obtain as a result of the Enterprise Technology project?

1192. Did the delivered product meet the specified requirements and goals of the Enterprise Technology project?

1193. How often did each stakeholder need an update?

5.4 Lessons Learned: Enterprise Technology

1194. How objective was the collection of data?

1195. Are the lessons more complex and multivariate?

1196. Was there a Enterprise Technology project Definition document. Was there a Enterprise Technology project Plan. Were they used during the Enterprise Technology project?

1197. How often did you violate the rules?

1198. What rewards do the individuals seek?

1199. How spontaneous are the communications?

1200. What is the impact of tax policy?

1201. How effective were your design reviews?

1202. Why do you need to measure?

1203. What are the expectations of the individuals?

1204. Do you have any real problems?

1205. How effective was the documentation that you received with the Enterprise Technology project product/service?

1206. How actively and meaningfully were

stakeholders involved in the Enterprise Technology project?

1207. What is the desired end-state?

1208. What is the frequency of group communications?

1209. How complete and timely were the materials you were provided to decide whether to proceed from one Enterprise Technology project lifecycle phase to the next?

1210. What is the growth stage of your organization?

1211. How effectively and consistently was sponsorship for the Enterprise Technology project conveyed?

1212. What was the methodology behind successful learning experiences, and how might they be applied to the broader challenge of your organizations knowledge management?

1213. What were the desired outcomes?

Index

ability 41, 87
absences   239
acceptable   47, 89, 150
acceptance   6, 120, 190, 258-259, 264
accepted   111
accepting   201, 263
access 2, 9-10, 23, 78, 219, 239, 262
accomplish   7, 94, 121, 123, 193, 200, 236, 241
accordance   263
according   32, 43
account   11, 44, 178, 238
accounted   51, 182
accounting   255
accounts   161, 197, 262
accrued   217
accuracy   60, 64, 184
accurate   10, 127, 167, 178, 181, 197
achievable   123, 200
achieve   7, 92, 95, 122, 130, 167, 195, 201, 212, 223, 253,
259
achieved   27, 85, 92, 114, 258
achieving   142, 208, 234, 254
acquire   226
acquired   165
across 62, 211
action 52, 56, 98, 101, 105-106, 136, 191, 206, 211, 251
actionable   54, 124
actioned   184
actions 26, 50, 99, 102, 118, 183, 208, 236
active 164
actively   203, 268
activities   20, 24, 84, 99-100, 120, 136, 163, 165-167, 169,
171-172, 175, 182-183, 185-186, 200, 207-208, 215, 220
activity 3-4, 33, 42, 143, 163, 165, 167-169, 171-173, 177, 182, 185-
186, 236, 260
actual 33, 55, 150, 161-162, 250, 256-257
actually   34, 77, 85, 100, 200, 253
actuals 215
adaptive   243
addition   8, 112

controlled   71, 148, 266
controls   22, 67, 73, 87, 92, 95, 97, 102, 104-106, 171, 213, 255, 263
convention   124
converge   249
convey   1
conveyed   269
cooperate   187
Copyright   1
correct46, 71, 97, 146, 181, 216
corrective   50, 102, 183
correspond   9, 11
costing50
counting   120, 165
countries   238
counts 120
course 41, 55, 252
covering   9, 106
coworker   131
craziest   124
create 11, 19, 77, 114, 120, 124, 156, 243
created   74, 79, 100, 139, 163, 202, 207, 219, 224, 246
creating   7, 57, 143, 156
creative   19
creativity   86
credible   187
crisis   25
criteria 2, 5, 9, 11, 34, 41, 44, 68, 84-85, 93, 108, 117, 131, 134, 146, 154, 156, 182, 188, 217, 221, 264
CRITERION   2, 17, 29, 46, 66, 81, 97, 109
critical 36-37, 44, 74, 95, 97, 107, 117, 135, 162, 166, 169, 178, 231-232, 243, 261
criticism   79
criticized   241
crucial 76, 178
crystal 13
cultural86
culture 41, 73, 143, 193, 199, 239, 243
current39, 46, 51, 59, 67, 71, 75, 87, 104, 113, 116, 119, 125, 128, 130, 157, 172, 198-199, 201, 207, 219, 223, 227, 238, 255, 260
currently   32, 111, 238, 250
custom27

immediate   51, 141, 208
impact 5, 32, 44, 48, 53, 55, 57-58, 61, 63, 84, 125, 143, 189-190,
207, 209-211, 228-229, 236, 244, 246, 268
impacted   136, 155, 158, 267
impacting   182
impacts   47, 50, 142, 158, 179, 205, 267
implement   26, 53, 74, 97, 150
implicit 130
import 141
important   18, 24, 38, 67, 75, 110, 113, 115-117, 125, 142,
191, 203, 222, 240-241
imprest 263
improve   2, 11-12, 81-82, 84-87, 90-95, 138, 158, 192-193,
216, 255, 260-261
improved   82, 84, 88-89, 105, 142, 218, 261
improving   91, 225
inactive   185
incentives   101, 242
include   26, 82, 94, 162, 166, 215, 217
included   2, 9, 21, 63, 143, 151, 162, 179, 185, 188, 217, 227,
256, 264
includes   10, 49, 148
including   22, 31, 33, 40, 47, 58, 72, 92, 98, 101, 158, 163,
244
increase   83, 127, 211, 250
increased   127
increasing   117, 232
incurred   63
in-depth   9, 12
indicate   47, 77, 103, 131, 198
indicated   102
indicators   19, 47, 55, 58, 67, 72, 75, 87, 98, 143, 162
indirect   55, 161-162, 185
indirectly   1
individual   1, 59, 136, 166, 181, 183, 198, 238, 240, 249, 266
industrial   212
industry   100, 121, 128, 164, 202, 219, 254
infinite 129
influence   85, 116, 135, 139, 232, 243-244, 267
inform 240
informal   248-249
informed   129, 197, 262
ingrained   103

nature 59, 217
nearest   13
necessary   48, 69-71, 77, 84, 111, 114, 123, 148, 157, 187,
212, 230, 246-247, 255, 263
needed   17-18, 20, 23-24, 26-27, 44, 67, 76, 79, 99, 106-107,
143, 147, 179, 186, 223-224, 245
negative   112
negatively   208, 223, 267
negotiate   131
negotiated   117, 263
neither 1
nervous   150
network   3, 171, 249
Neutral 12, 17, 29, 46, 66, 81, 97, 109
normal 103
notice 1, 262-263
noticing   231
notified   264
number   28, 45, 65, 80, 96, 108, 133, 167, 176, 211, 238,
262, 270
numbers   110, 177, 238
numerous   265
objection   22, 24
objective   7, 53, 141-142, 156, 162, 189, 231, 246, 268
objectives   24, 27, 29, 35-36, 79, 101, 108, 111, 113, 128, 131,
146, 157, 181, 191, 203, 207-208, 216, 225, 234, 243, 254
Observe   233
observed   82
Observer   233
obsolete   129
obstacles   21, 179, 188
obtain 124, 267
obtained   40, 62, 157
obtaining   57
obvious   240
obviously   13
occurring   93
occurs 25, 53, 107, 143
offerings   75, 91
office   216, 225, 264
officers 218
officials 264
one-time   7

CPSIA information can be obtained
at www.ICGtesting.com
Printed in the USA
BVHW041435110719
553202BV00011B/508/P